I

# Also by Jared McCann

*Marked for Judgment*

*The Dead Will Rise*

# FOREVER I WILL BE

2018 JDM Books Paperback

Copyright © July 2018 by Jared McCann

Printed in the United States of America

Cover Design: Jared McCann


McCann, Jared

(Poems)

Forever I Will Be / Jared McCann

ISBN 13: 978-0692142646

ISBN 10: 0692142649


*Bible passages are taken from the NLT (New Living Translation)*
*Bible*
Life Application Study Bible, Second Edition. Illinois. Tyndale
House Publishers, 2004

# FOREVER I WILL BE

## JARED MCCANN

ł

JDM BOOKS + OHIO

*For everyone*

*Kiss me and kiss me again,*
*for your love is sweeter than wine.*

*Love flashes like fire,*
*the brightest kind of flame.*
*Many waters cannot quench love,*
*nor can rivers drown it.*

## Song of Songs 1:2 & 8:6-7

*Make it your goal to live a quiet life,*
*minding your own business*
*and working with your hands.*

## 1 Thessalonians 4:11

# Contents

## The Love Poems

# The Other Poems

XIV

# FOREVER I WILL BE

# My Love For You

*This is one of my very first poems that I wrote when I started, I believe, maturing as a poet. We all want to be loved, and this poem reaches deep down inside to the heart of a man who loves a woman to the fullest. Love has many respective forms, but this one is dedicated to the intense love that a man has for a woman.*

# My Love For You

*My love for you I hold within my heart forever*
*the love I've held for you no one can sever.*
*But you're in a relationship with someone else on your mind*
*I've tried, but forgetting you I could never leave behind.*
*Deep down I think you still have feelings for me*
*but don't want to reveal your secrets and what you really see.*
*My love for you I hold inside my soul even after my demise*
*heart stops each and every time I look into your eyes.*
*Your gaze expresses the love I've been searching for*
*your beauty and personality are precious that I can't ignore.*
*I was too blind to see the love you had for me long ago*
*now my eyes see the light again and all that I know*
*is that my love for you is true and cannot be broken*
*I see your love now that I have awoken.*
*Thinking about you all the time when nobody else is around*
*my love for you is everlasting in which cannot be battered down.*
*I found your love once, I will find it again*
*in the past we had love but forever that has been.*
*Back then I broke our love, I'm the one to blame*
*I've changed but my love for you is still the same.*
*Every time I look at you I end up in a daze*
*my love is here for you forever and always.*
*Your name will always speak through the shining weather*
*my love for you I hold within my heart forever.*

*6/29/2005*

# If You Need

*I wrote this poem about a man who loves a woman and is there for her, with the woman realizing the love of her life is right in front of her. To me, poetry is a lot like fiction. I try to write short stories that will interest my reader and leave them contemplating about what they just read. Love is one of those major topics, and I'm not ashamed to speak of something so moving and powerful.*

# If You Need

$M$y love, my heart, my comfort will forever be true
if you need a friend and lover I'm here for you.
Lonesome laying around alone late at night
if you need someone then I will hold you tight.
The closeness and love that you yearn for and miss
if you need me I'm that person you can hug and kiss.
Saddened, no one to pick you up to get you through
if you need someone it's me that you can talk to.
Tell me your feelings, your secrets, I'll be your man
if you need a close friend it is I who will understand.
Companionless, but you're such a beautiful queen
if you need me for life then surely I'm your king.
Good lovin' you've searched for that no one can sever
if you need me I'm the one you should be with forever.
Needing someone to embrace, holding you high above
never letting you go by always giving you all of my love.

11/?/2005

# *Just So You Know*

*Just So You Know has always been one of my favorite poems that I wrote. It's basically stating that a man loves his woman so much that he's always there for her, sacrificing for her, fighting for her, and reminding her that all he is belongs to her. Now these three remain: faith, hope, and love. But the greatest of these is love. Men, love your wife or girlfriend like she's the only one.*

# Just So You Know

*Baby this love I feel for you deep inside*
*releases my soul with my heart open wide.*
*Before you my life was troubled and hollow*
*always by your side, wherever you go I'm bound to follow.*
*If ever you were down I will be there to brighten your day*
*or if you were heartbroken I will be there to kiss your tears away.*
*For some reason if you were lonesome during the night*
*you mustn't worry for I'll be there to hold you tight.*
*Giving you all of my love, everything I do is only for you*
*your mind, body, beauty, oh how I utterly adore you.*
*You're my angel who spreads her wings beyond the sky*
*having you in my life, I must be the world's most fortunate guy.*
*I yearned to try to find a way to make ends meet*
*when our lips connect I can lovingly feel the heat*
*that we create as our hearts together intertwine*
*forever in this life I am yours just as you are mine.*
*I shall always fight for you, for you are my lover*
*you're all I need, I could never ever want another.*
*Just wanted to tell you this just so you know*
*that my heart is yours and that I love you so.*

*5/13/2006*

# How Long ?

*I wrote this poem how two lovers can long for one another with being away from each other. Though the love inside burns within, miles apart - emotionally speaking - strains them until they meet again. While away, the man reminisces about their relationship and is hoping the woman is doing something similar. As the popular song goes, sometimes "waiting is the hardest part."*

# How Long ?

Missing you day and night
as I look up at the stars all alone.
Wondering if you're looking up at the same sky
thinking of me even though we're in different zones.

Your touch, your warmth
the way you make me feel inside.
Heartache sets in with you away
my love for you I will not hide.

At the airport we kissed
as if it were our last time.
We didn't want to let each other go
I am yours, and you are mine.

In the midst of your absence
I am but a man with a bleeding heart.
Desperately waiting for your return
for without you I'm broken down and cannot start.

Romantic nights filled with passion
and a fire not meant to go out.
Giving you my all and loving you the rest of my life
now that's what I'm all about.

Until then I pray I dream of you every night
with you being gone.
The nights spent alone are killing me and I'm tired of guessing:
when will you return to me my love? How long?

11/14/2016

# The Convening Path

With The Convening Path, I place lovers in this fantasy world where a love relationship awaits all, whether that's reconnecting or finding true love for the first time. I'm a fan of certain fantasy - The Hobbit and The Lord of the Rings Trilogies - and so I chose to create my own little world in this poem where love abounds and is made for all.

# The Convening Path

*There's a path where loved ones reunite*
*a place where it's never cloudy but always light.*
*Meeting again with the one who got away*
*walking together down the path on a beautiful day.*
*It's a place where colorful leaves fall from trees*
*and smiles never fade through the pleasant breeze.*
*A path where dreams come true and close loves intertwine*
*searching for that special person, this is the path where you combine.*
*Lovingly feels like Heaven, this place, this path*
*where you're free to run, to kiss, to laugh.*
*In this world sunsets are divine and hearts are not broken*
*but where they come together and fly into the open.*
*Beyond this path is a field overflowing with mirth*
*out there somewhere is this place where love got its birth.*
*The charming field is where the two become one*
*dancing and holding each other, shining in the sun.*
*This path, this field, all resemble unbelievable dreams*
*but it's real, where everything is as genuine as it seems.*
*Here hearts reconvene and love is always flowing*
*this path I'm looking highly forward to going.*

*9/6/2005*

# Missing Smile

*We humans are heartbroken when we feel the love of our life has gone out of our lives. It changes us, saddens us, and fractures our spirit for a time. I wrote Missing Smile with how a man can feel when his love is now out of the picture. His mood is down, his heart aches, and he turns into somebody no one knows anymore. Harold Melvin sang it best in "All Because Of A Woman."*

# Missing Smile

*People* wonder what happened to the real and old me
they're confused about how I've come to be.
They ask others what happened to his face and his smile
sorry to say but it's flown away for a long while.
Missing my kindness and my loving personality
people long for my gentleness, my honesty, my mentality.
Everyone asks, "Why has he changed, it seems so weird?"
I'll tell you my secret why all this has disappeared.
I've been saddened, it's all because of a girl
she was beautiful and hard to find, like a pearl.
Words cannot express the bond that we had
now that she's gone I'm all lonely and sad.
Thinking of her as I listen to my favorite love tune
wishing that her and I can be together soon.
Believing that the two of us belonged to each other
to find one like her, I will never see another.
That's why I'm lost and because of the sudden change
until I see her again I will not in any way rearrange.
Missing her so much, without her I'm in denial
it's because of her that I no more wear my smile.

*8/22/2005*

# *For Your Eyes Only*

*A simple poem, For Your Eyes Only has always been one of my favorite romance poems that I've written. That's the way these moments should be with your spouse, For Your Eyes Only, not for anyone else. To add, we should only have eyes for our spouse and not be looking with lust to that of another.*

# For Your Eyes Only

*Everything we do tonight I do only for you*
*keep it a secret all the romantic things that we do.*
*I've never loved anybody like you in my life before*
*caress my lips as I take your clothes off and toss them to the floor.*
*Your hands feel my body with a pleasurable touch*
*I'll hold you all night since we won't be sleeping much.*
*Your eyes are like a flame sparkling in a fire*
*looking into them I see nothing but love and desire.*
*Embrace me with your irresistible body all night*
*I'll do whatever you want, just do me right.*
*You drive me crazy, I can't help my temptation*
*our love for one another, I treasure the sensation.*
*Tonight you won't have to worry about being lonely*
*everything we do and see is for your eyes only.*

*6/15/2005*

# The Kiss

*Do you remember your first kiss? I do, and it was bad. But I was young and didn't have a clue what I was doing. Whether a "peck" on the cheek or a quick one on the lips, sometimes kisses can be taken for granted. But when given to the one who you truly love, it is a shared connection that feels amazing.*

# The Kiss

*The kiss we shared I shall endlessly keep memory of*
*our connection was an exquisite, inner love.*

*The taste of your voluptuous lips was so luscious*
*inside my heart was beating rapidly with tempting rushes.*

*My lips entwined with yours tasted very sweet*
*the longing for our kiss was sensuous and complete.*

*Our bodies filled with bliss as we breathed into each other's soul*
*wishing our kiss was everlasting it was harmonious and whole.*

*The kiss - oh our kiss - I yearn for more each and every night*
*craving your tongue, for it was such a delight.*

*All I ever think of is you as the world turns*
*my hunger for you is desperate, and it burns.*

*Our ecstatic moment I will evermore treasure and miss*
*but forever I will always remember our intimate kiss.*

*8/16/2005*

# I Wonder

*This poem is about longing for the person you miss and who you can't wait to see again. It's about not knowing for sure when they're going to show up in your life again, but you're certain they're going to at some point, or at least you hope. Traveling into my youth, I Wonder makes me think of girl crushes I used to have, thinking they were the "only ones." I laugh as I reminisce.*

# I Wonder

*I* wonder if again I will see your captivating face
we will see each other again whatever the case.
Missing your closeness and your mellifluous voice
I must see you again, I do not have a choice.
Was very hard but you and I had to go away
envision you inside my head each and every day.
No matter how much the time, we will find one another again
always remembering our lasting moments no matter how long it has been.
You and I seemed to be the perfect pair
you were the one and affectionately fair.
The day we see again will be breathtaking and intense
then our fondness will reconvene and it will all make sense.
I can picture us spending the rest of our lives together
never letting go again but will love each other forever.
Our desire and memories we keep no one can ever sunder
when and how soon will we see again is all I can wonder.

*8/9/2005*

# A Heart Searching For Love

*To me, A Heart Searching For Love is finally realizing you're ready for a committed and faithful relationship that results in marriage. Back in high school, I barely dated and had no clue what a relationship was. I knew though, at the time and when I matured, that I was ready to give my heart to a woman in an all-serious, devoted way - hand in hand in marriage.*

# A Heart Searching For Love

*It's the feeling one gets when love is stored for that special soul
the love that one must release so that their heart will be whole.
Searching for that Heavenly love that will complete one's dreams
daydreaming of your love where it's as true as it seems.
This celestial feeling of love for this person is everlasting
where the two hearts join and memories are never passing.
Words cannot describe the bond between the two
envisioning the romantic day when the couple will give life to new.
Endlessly being faithful, till death the pair won't part
the love will forever be safe deep within the heart.
It is this feeling where the spirit rises high above
it is this feeling where there is a heart searching for love.*

*12/12/2005*

# The Date

*Easily stated, The Date is about going on a date with the one you want, specifically your very first date. The nervousness builds inside, you're wondering if they're "into you," the anticipation of a kiss grows, you're making sure you don't have any "boogers" hanging out (Haha!)...etc. One of my early poems and one I'm fond of, The Date is a feel-good poem.*

# The Date

*B*uy *a beautiful flower*
*turn on the power*
*to the shower*
*got to get ready within the hour.*
*I can't wait because tonight's my big date*
*but I have to hurry and not be late.*
*Dress up nice and put on some cologne*
*I then pick up the phone*
*to make sure we're still on tonight*
*she says to me, "That's exactly right!"*
*Outside her house ringing her bell*
*we're going to have a fun time I can tell.*
*Opening up she looks so hot*
*looking at her I can't stop.*
*Thinking of her makes me want her more*
*walking side by side, I then open for her my truck door.*
*Tonight I'm taking her out to eat at a nice place*
*staring at her makes my heart race.*
*This evening I love how she did her hair*
*arriving at the restaurant, I push in her chair.*
*After eating we go to the movie theater*
*glancing at her, I'm so fortunate that I've gotten to meet her.*
*Then we visit the mall and have some fun*
*spending time with her makes me love her a ton.*
*Next we stop and have some ice cream*
*to me she's like an unbelievable dream.*
*It's getting late, so the two of us head home*
*just me and her all alone.*

*This night never once went bad*
*as we discuss about how much fun we had.*
*Everything tonight went as planned*
*I then build up the courage and take her hand.*
*She massages my hand quite a bit*
*with her loveable touch she caresses it.*
*Driving up her driveway*
*thinking how we both had such a great day.*
*We had a wonderful night with all the time we took*
*as I look over at her she's giving me that look.*
*The time we had together I'm going to miss*
*then she reaches over and gives me a kiss.*
*I pull her back for a kiss one more time*
*happy and grateful that she is all mine.*
*We stop because we came to a limit*
*we are mute and don't talk for a minute.*
*She says, "I really like you"*
*I say, "I do too."*
*She gave me another kiss and said thanks for the time*
*also for the ride*
*closing her door, I drive away with nothing to hide*
*with that tingling, passionate feeling inside.*

*2002 or 2003*

*Manhattan, a beloved Black Labrador, blessed my life for many years. We were extremely close, and she lived a long life of 14 years before developing seizures, believed to be the result of a brain tumor. A favorite picture of her and I, I still miss her dearly but cherish the span of life we were able to spend together.*

# Ready For Love

*Whether a bad break up, a divorce, or ready to begin a relationship, Ready For Love is about taking that leap of faith to start over again, giving someone that chance to see if it will go further, or looking to find love for the first time. Though I broke a couple hearts back in the day (sorry to those girls who I did), I knew when the time was when I was Ready For Love.*

# Ready For Love

*I've reminisced about this and thought a lot*
*thinking of the signs surrounding me and all that I've got.*
*It took some time but I've decided that I'm ready for love*
*ready for someone's comfort to come and take me up above.*
*Seeking day and night but love for me was hidden*
*to me it felt like attachment was out of sight and forbidden.*
*Then the light shined through my heart*
*ready for love I was destined to start.*
*I've found the perfect someone to ease my essence*
*to delete the pain with their healing presence.*
*This individual to my heart will bring harmony and restoration*
*our affection is bold, and very strong will be our love's new creation.*
*My life is now abundant with solace and compassion*
*for our love is portrayed in absolute romantic fashion.*
*I'm now ready for love after searching for a long time*
*ready for my love and someone else's to come in and twine.*

*7/31/2005*

# When I Do Find You

*Ever been separated from someone (not separated as split up but separated as distance), only to realize that that's the person who you truly want to be with? That's what When I Do Find You is all about. Not realizing the strong relationship you had with someone until they're away, but then coming to the conclusion that, when you do find them again, you're holding on to them.*

# When I Do Find You

*Separated only shortly, so I mustn't worry*
*even though I have time I want to hurry*
*for I'm missing you and your nearness*
*the things I need to tell you, I can't wait till you hear this.*
*Expressing my feelings for you face to face*
*memories we keep I shall not ever misplace.*
*You caressed my heart with your tender touch*
*I truly and surely need you in my life so much.*
*When we see each other again I'm embracing you in my arms*
*my feelings and affection for you is indescribable, it never harms.*
*Reliving our past when we would look into each other's eyes and gaze*
*this time we're keeping one another for the future, until the end of days.*
*The time spent together and all that we've been through*
*we will both be warmhearted again when I do find you.*

*9/13/2005*

# Anything For You

*Willing to do anything that is right, honorable, and faithful for the one you're with? That's how I feel about a relationship with a woman/marriage. Knowing we are no longer two but one, united in marriage, I am willing to sacrifice and uphold what marriage stands for in the eyes of God. I'd be blessed with a good and loving wife, and I'd be willing to do anything for her, as long as it's good and right.*

# *Anything For You*

*B*aby I love the things you do
that's why I'll do anything for you.
Spending time with you is the best
I never want to give you a rest.
Whatever you want I'm willing to buy
because I'm gonna keep on loving you till the day I die.
For you mean everything to me
because we're together forever you see.
If ever you're tired out and stressed
then lay your weary head on my chest.
I can't get you out of my mind
for your love is special and the best kind.
I love how you say I'm a "cutey"
words will never explain your beauty.
Picturing us husband and wife
because I want to love you the rest of my life.
Reminiscing about me and you
thinking how we make a perfect two.
I love how you act and how you are
you mean more to me than any shining star.
Can't wait to spend our lives together
because I'm loving and keeping you forever.

*2002 or 2003*

# Long Way Home

*Long Way Home is all about enjoying every second with the one your heart melts over. Even though I'm not a big country music fan, this poem reminds me of a country song: a bed of a pickup truck, a gravel road, a starlit night, crickets and fireflies, etc. One of my favorite love poems, I truly enjoyed writing every word of Long Way Home.*

# Long Way Home

*S*eniors in high school, but I feel like we're married
*what's it been, two years that we've been together?*
*Our hearts belong to no one else, even though we're young*
*with you in my life, you bring the fairest of weather.*


*W*e leave the party early, for neither of us are "drinkers"
*taking you by the hand, we walk out into the starlit night.*
*Stopping, you turn toward me with the face of an angel*
*kissing me, the way you're making me feel is so right.*


*O*pening the door, you sit in the passenger seat
*behind the wheel I start my truck up, and off we go.*
*Driving, you move closer, clinging to my side and kissing my neck*
*out in the country we pull over, as we start to take things slow.*


*T*he sound of rustling leaves and crickets fills the air
*through the open windows a soothing breeze feels fine.*
*Feeling one another and kissing, my heart is on fire*
*like wine you taste sweet, and you are all mine.*


*O*ur bodies are hungry for the other, stimulating sexual urges
*not wanting to go any further, we've been here before.*
*Even though it's hard, we believe in marriage and in "waiting"*
*we let up, but my lips and tongue, you can have some more.*

*S*preading out a blanket, you lay next to me in the bed of my truck
looking up, hanging high and pale is the brilliance of the moon.
The aroma of your long dark hair and perfume fills my lungs
your dad's gonna kill me, we have to get up and get going soon.


*B*ack on the gravel road, the stones crunch underneath the tires
the fireflies are out, but their beauty doesn't compare to you.
You say, "I love you. I want to be with you forever"
looking at you, enjoying the view, I say, "I love you too."


*P*ulling into your driveway, your parents left the front porch light on
kissing me good night, I am your man, and my heart you own.
At the front door you turn around, your smile shines bright
tonight I loved our time alone, and that we took the long way home.

*3/15/2017*

*This woman right here, my Grandma Arck, has had such a tremendous impact in my life. From reading me Bible stories as a child, all the way to supporting and loving me with her whole heart, my grandmother is an angel to me. Enjoying every conversation and moment with her that I can, I love her dearly!*

# *Just A Dream*

*All of us have dreams. Some we like and some we dislike, but we can't control them. Just A Dream enters the sleeping mind of a repentant man who will do anything to reclaim the love that he had with the woman he loves. After apologizing and crying, love and relationship is restored, but at the climax of the moment, the man awakens and realizes it was Just A Dream.*

# *Just A Dream*

*I dreamt of our love reuniting again*
*it was so intense, never caused any sin.*
*The reason we separated was because of our fight*
*but I'm prepared to change and set things right.*
*Now our love has joined and it seems so real*
*I wish you could only perceive how I feel.*
*My head is flooded with all our charming memories*
*I see myself weeping and apologizing on my knees.*
*Begging for you to come and take me back*
*sorry about the devotion which I seem to lack.*
*Without you my heart and life is not complete*
*you're a part of me, from my head to my feet.*
*You sob but are an accepting person*
*never again will I let our love worsen.*
*Running, you throw your arms around my chest*
*I can breathe again, my body filling with zest.*
*I look into your teary eyes as you look into mine*
*you pull my head over for a kiss as our lips combine.*
*We're whole again as we love one another throughout the night*
*the darkness is now gone, for our yearning has produced light.*
*My soul is full of joy, deep down inside I'm wholehearted*
*in the beginning I wish our passion never had parted.*
*Our love will live on forever, however that may seem*
*then I realize that I have awoken to only a dream.*

*7/27/2005*

# You Wanna Be With Me

*As people, we oftentimes know we want to be with somebody, but sometimes something is holding us back. What? Many things I'm not going into detail in. You Wanna Be With Me expresses the feelings a man has for a woman who he knows wants him. He's ready for her, but doesn't want to waste his time if she only wants to be a friend, because he's ready to offer her all he is.*

# You Wanna Be With Me

Come here baby and lay by my side
your feelings no more you have to hide.
Loving the truth that you wanna be with me
together forever is how we were meant to be.
Let us join together just as a suture
exit the past and come into my future.
With me baby you shall never feel confined
all I want is to place that love feeling in your mind.
The distance between us I am truly hating
until we're together I am here for you waiting.
Waiting for you to come and take me by the hand
knowing you wanna be with me, baby I'm your man.
If love is real then you ought to be with me
until I die this very thing is a certainty.
Wanting you, but if all you want is to be a friend of mine
I'll be honest baby, I don't even wanna waste my time.
Cause I wanna kiss you right, hug you tight
love you each and every night.

2/9/2007

# *Always With You*

*Whether divided by distance, time, or death, Always With You reassures someone that you're always in their heart. While living, we can take people with us in spirit. As a Christian, I believe in life after death, and those who remain in the faith can know that their loved one - father, mother, son, daughter, sibling, friend, etc. - resides within and is always with them.*

# *Always With You*

*No matter how far you go*
*whether it be high or low*
*please don't feel sad with woe.*
*I'll be inside your heart forever*
*through the good and bad weather*
*truly deep inside we'll always be together.*
*It saddens me to see you leave*
*but I'm going to do my best not to grieve*
*we will rejoin again, you must believe.*
*Remember when we wrote our initials on that tree?*
*if you're distressed just close your eyes, that's where I'll be*
*or if you're lonely and down just think of me.*
*Nothing comes before you, you're first*
*your departing, nothing could be worse*
*but our love for each other no one can burst.*
*The rest of my life I love you with a passion*
*delighted that I received your satisfaction*
*tears come to my eyes, I can't help my reaction.*
*It's hard for me but each and every day*
*I'll think of you every time I lay*
*I wish that you never had to go away.*
*You always will love me and will always stay true*
*without you I don't know really what to do*
*but inside our hearts I'll always be with you.*

*8/5/2005*

# *LOVE*

*There's just something about the word "love." It makes us feel good, it shows we care, and it's good medicine for the heart. Love is a human emotion that we all want to feel. Though it has many definitions, I'm referring to the kind of love we should have for our fellow man and woman, a love that looks attractive on the outside that draws people closer, so all can share in its fullness.*

# *LOVE*

*L*ove as if there is no tomorrow by

*O*pening your heart to love <u>always</u>.

*V*alue love so the world may see

*E*verybody embracing love for all of <u>days</u>.

*1/2/2006*

# Life Without You

*Once in high school and a younger man, I wrote from our world's perspective in certain ways. Skewed relationships as seen or written in movies, TV shows, and books – unfortunately - is part of the world we live in, portraying a false image of true love that others deem acceptable per the world's vision. Not approving of this kind of lifestyle, Life Without You is about broken/bad relationships and moving on.*

# Life Without You

*T*ears flowing, heart broken, love gone astray,
head down, lost, walking around lonesome every day.
Our love was warm only to fade away cold
my heart given to you which you could not hold.
Days and nights filled with romance and heat
life without you, sadly mine is no longer sweet.
Kisses filled with bliss, hugs of warmth, a love in the making
the end conclusion: it was my heart that you were breaking.
Trying to forget, but you linger inside of my mind
turning your back in the dark, leaving me behind.
Giving you my all, up high I held you way above
what I wouldn't do to again feel and taste your love.
Knowing I won't, it's time that I found love anew
to get over you and all that I've had to go through.
My tears will dry, head will hold high, and my heart will repair
entwining with another's to form a deep and lovely pair.
A love relationship will arise and the romance will return
you used to be all I needed, but with love you have much to learn.
Walking hand in hand with another, thinking for a minute
my life is now complete and very happy without you in it.

*8/28/2007*

# The Girl

*Men, remember seeing the girl of your dreams, who you couldn't stop thinking about, and who you knew was "the one?" This poem, The Girl, sums it all up. That's the way a man should feel about the woman he loves: thinking she's beautiful, excited to grow old with her, doing anything and just having a good time with her, and oh, I must add this day in age, being faithful only to her.*

# *The Girl*

*Seeing the girl of my dreams walk before me*
*she's so beautiful and great you see*
*she unlocks my heart with her passionate key.*
*When I look into her eyes*
*I know that she is my prize*
*because I want to be with her until it's my demise.*
*I love the way she likes to dress*
*someday I hope I can provide for her much caress*
*if she wanted to do something with me I would say "yes!"*
*What I wouldn't do for one kiss*
*that would be my biggest wish*
*filling her life with absolute bliss.*
*I would do anything for her*
*because she is so very pure*
*if ever I was sick she would be my cure.*
*I can picture us together*
*until the end of time forever*
*because she will always be my lovely weather.*
*She will be my "Hon"*
*we're going to have so much fun*
*because I know that she is the one.*

*2002 or 2003*

# *When ?*

*Ever feel lonesome, wondering if Mr. or Mrs. Right is out there somewhere for you? This poem, When, is about someone ready to be with that "someone", but also knowing that it could take some time or that it may not even come at all. So many times in life we see others rush into relationships or just "settle" for what's there at the time, but with patience, sometimes waiting pays off.*

# *When ?*

*Seeking on my engaging journey West, South, East, and North*
*longing always but when is the love of my life going to come forth?*

*Craving while looking for love on a puzzling quest*
*confused about what love truly is and how it's expressed.*

*Will I be stranded in the dark or will I shine?*
*will love forever be lost or will it be mine?*

*Not knowing but the future one day reveals*
*if I will receive love and how it passionately feels.*

*Stories filled with love - sorry to say I have none*
*but I thought there was that one special person for every one?*

*This picture of me forever being lonesome, I hate it*
*can't stand the pain of being set apart and isolated.*

*Even though I've come upon so much heartache and so much strife*
*I'm going to continue my journey searching for the love of my life.*

*12/15/2005*

# Sea Of Love

*Sea Of Love was one of those poems I wrote that I could visualize vividly in my head: a picturesque beach setting, a sandy shore, waves crashing, a setting sun, and two lovers holding one another in the middle of it all. For some reason writing about love and a beach environment just seems to go hand in hand, so I wrote Sea Of Love hoping you can picture your own love/beach scene.*

# Sea Of Love

*Sun setting in the midst of the open sea*
*holding you closely by my side.*
*Walking lovingly the sandy shore of the beach*
*romantically kissing my gorgeous bride.*

*Seducing me with your beauty*
*with your body wrapped around mine.*
*Roaming up the stairway to the silk sheeted bed*
*our love tastes sweeter than any kind of wine.*

*Irresistible lovemaking through the pleasant ocean breeze*
*creates an arousing sensation that sends me soaring.*
*Two pairs of eyes affixed to one another's*
*with you in my life love never gets boring.*

*A night full of love stays in my mind*
*with morning sun rays gleaming through the balcony's curtain.*
*Our close relationship and endless love*
*I want you always in my life babe, I'm certain.*

*5/2/2008*

# The One Who Got Away

*So many movies dramatize love that is lost. With scenes of anticipation, usually the other person comes back and love is once again reunited; but, in the real world, this isn't always true. The One Who Got Away travels back to a love relationship that was strong, only to be lost and unsure if it will ever be found again. An exhortation: if you find true love, don't let it get away.*

# The One Who Got Away

*Thinking of you as my eyes overflow with tears*
*if we were to unite again, would it be days, months, years?*
*Then the question arises if I will ever see you again*
*the countless memories, without you where do I begin?*
*When I said I loved you it is what I meant*
*you loved me back for you were Heaven sent.*
*Heartbroken, my heart cannot beat without you in it*
*come retrieve it, you're the only one I allow to win it.*
*In constant discomfort me living my life without you*
*frequently crying for your return, there's nothing I can do.*
*Until the day of my demise it is you who I forever will miss*
*your presence, love, the lips that gave me many a kiss.*
*Eternally reminiscing of our love and relationship every day*
*not wanting anybody else, for you were my love that got away.*

*12/16/2005*

# Daydream

*We daydream of so much: relationships, our futures, where we want to be years from now, what it would be like to be in certain situations, etc. In particular, Daydream is about thinking of that someone who you want to be with real bad. They're always on your mind, and no matter how hard you try, you can't get them out of it; and you can't wait until you see them again.*

# Daydream

*Daydreaming of you always inside my head*
*fantasizing, I think of you in my dreams every night in bed.*
*Looking up at the clouds I end up in a daze*
*thinking of you inside of my mind always.*
*You portray such a beautiful sight through my eyes*
*keeping faith in seeing you again before my demise.*
*I see you being my girl and me being your man*
*walking along a sunny beach hand in hand.*
*A smile widens across my lips when I think of you*
*with you my life was depicted with a lovely hue.*
*Seeing you made my days a lot brighter*
*needing you because I'm a lover, not a fighter.*
*I was alive and happy with you, I felt so real*
*no one could ever understand how you made me feel.*
*So I will always daydream of you day in and day out*
*you showed me what pleasure is truly all about.*
*Our stories were filled with joy and happiness, no strife*
*when again are you going to show up in my life?*

*8/11/2005*

# *Turn Away*

*The story of Turn Away is kind of like a shaky relationship, similar to many relationships today. The man in this poem can't Turn Away or get over the woman who he truly loves, even though their situation isn't the way they'd hoped it would be. Makes me think of our human relationships. How often we won't give up or stop fighting for the one person who we deeply love.*

# Turn Away

*I've tried but I can't seem to turn away from you*
*your love was passionate and irresistibly true.*
*We were inseparable, that's what you used to say*
*your inviting smile made for a brighter day.*
*Our fondness for one another was unbreakable*
*let's get back together, I know that we're capable.*
*When I look at you my heart starts to race*
*remember and loved kissing your beloved face.*
*With arms wide open I need you in my life*
*reminiscing when we said we would be husband and wife.*
*We've set apart but I still have that same feeling for you*
*you and I can erase our old relationship and make it new.*
*I'll always keep memory of our first kiss*
*deeply and wholeheartedly it is you who I miss.*
*Surely inside your heart you feel the same*
*never again will I cause you any pain.*
*Those summer days being with each other all the time*
*holding you in my arms, thankful that you were all mine.*
*I will never turn my back on you on any given day*
*let us relive our love and attachment, there has to be a way.*

*6/11/2005*

# Away With The Past

*Bad past relationships have affected many. Away With The Past is for those people. Many have a hard time being involved with someone else given their past experiences. But the past needs to be forgotten and the present lived. There are good people out there, but you need to be patient and not just settle for someone quick. P.S., there's nothing wrong with being single either.*

# *Away With The Past*

*I*'*ve tried and tried but my feelings for you will never slip away*
*no matter how hard they remain in my mind each and every day.*
*It has taken you a while, but at last*
*it's time for you to restart, leaving the past.*
*You've seen too much darkness, now it's time to shine*
*time for you to love me so that I may make you mine.*
*The love is there, it just needs to conspire*
*to warm the heart and soul, just as a fire.*
*You want me deep within, but are sadly confused*
*about your past and how you used to be abused.*
*Living for the love of you, I long for your gaze*
*offering nothing but love and happiness for all of your days.*
*Whether times are good, bad, happy, or sad*
*I'm here through all the hard times you've had.*
*We should be together just as the sun shines high above*
*let me into your world, filling it with continuous love.*
*You belong to me just as I belong to you*
*we love this fact, knowing that it is true.*
*Just as the summer breeze sweeps across the land*
*be away with the past so that I may be your man.*

*2/3/2007*

# Even Though We're Friends

*I can remember in my younger days and even now seeing it with adults, those people who claim to be friends but you can tell by the way they are around each other that they mean more than that. Even Though We're Friends was written to take that step from a friendship relationship toward a love relationship. Or in this poem's case, reigniting a relationship that once was.*

# Even Though We're Friends

*The beautiful sunny days and all your lovely ways*
*make me think of you as I reminisce in a daze.*
*A relationship we once had was strong, but ended weak*
*wondering if we can relight our flame, it's your love I seek.*
*Even though we're friends we still hold hands and kiss*
*lost without you, oh woman I wish you only understood this.*
*The urge to be with you only continues to grow*
*is this path we're taking right? I do not know.*
*You pretend to not want me even though you really do*
*let's end these mind games, all I need is you.*
*Even in public gorgeous lady you act as if I was your man*
*my love is yours, so come take it baby, I'm your biggest fan.*
*Deep within that heart of yours you know you're mine*
*me holding you, you kissing me, makes us feel fine.*
*Don't hide it, your love for me is all in your eyes*
*my one wish: to have you be my woman till my demise.*

*11/27/2007*

# Rewind

*A lot of us wonder at times what could've been if we would've stayed together with someone. Or, we wish we could go back and appreciate and embrace a relationship or love that we once had. This poem, Rewind, reflects on that. Although we can't change the past, most of the time things just seem to work out better for the good. So much better than what we ourselves could've planned.*

# *Rewind*

*You* *enabled me to feel something so special*
*that deep within me it felt purely <u>divine</u>.*
*Searching for a way for us to reconvene*
*knowing there's a way again I will make you <u>mine</u>.*

*You* *wanted me to be yours*
*just as I wanted you to be <u>mine</u>.*
*A shooting star passed when I thought of you*
*this must be a <u>sign</u>.*

*Even* *though our days are numbered*
*it is you forever I will continue to <u>find</u>.*
*Dreaming of inside my mind as*
*I cherished how our affection <u>intertwined</u>.*

*In* *this life or in the next*
*we will rejoin as our love will <u>combine</u>.*
*Your lips tasted sweet as honey*
*and angelic as of the greatest <u>wine</u>.*

*Yearning* *for your love and body*
*every night as your memory lives within my <u>mind</u>.*
*Wanting you by my side every day*
*it is time that I only wish I could <u>rewind</u>.*

*12/31/2005*

63

# Eternal Love

*This poem I wrote with the deepest respect and faithfulness a man can have for his wife. With marriage in mind, Eternal Love is dedicating your heart and soul wholeheartedly to your spouse and to none other. God intends marriage to be permanent while we're alive, through the good and bad times. Since husband and wife are no longer two but one, it's imperative we do all in our power to keep this bond holy.*

# Eternal Love

*T*he best of me comes out when I'm with you lady
for your love is radiant and never to be shady.
When I'm with you my heart rate ascends high above
I feel as if I'm in Heaven being enveloped in your love.
Tonight I want to lie you down and love you like never before
good lovemaking all through the night, as I close the bedroom door.
Embraced in my arms is an angel who is my soul mate
two hearts destined for eternal love, this must be fate.
Gentle kisses and tender touching fill the room full of light
the sensual urge grows as our yearning soars to a celestial height.
Together as one, this feeling is the most amazing ever felt
the heat our intimacy conceives makes my heart want to melt.
As I look into my lover's eyes I want us to make a vow
that we'll love each other always, even when the times get foul.
Our kiss will seal the oath, for this love between us is forever
everlasting, in which even the most powerful force could not sever.
Just know baby that I love you and that I'm yours always
being with you lover is how I want to spend the rest of my days.

*1/17/2008*

# Summer Beach Romance

*With Summer Beach Romance, I give you my final love poem of this book. Ironically, this was also the last love poem I wrote. A longer romance poem and attempting to save one of the best for last, Summer Beach Romance is definitely one of my top favorites. You can place yourself in this sun-filled, oceanic setting and get lost in this story of two people growing closer together in love. Going out with a bow, I hope you've enjoyed these love poems. Now come join me for The Other Poems!*

# Summer Beach Romance

*A bad breakup a few months ago has me flying*
*down to The Outer Banks where the sun sets are never dying*
*relationships?, let me tell you, I'm about to stop trying.*

*But little did I know it would be here where I found love*
*the woman I fell for had to be an angel sent from above*
*it was here where I spread my wings, just like a dove.*

*The beach house I rented had a breathtaking view of the sea*
*a feel-good breeze and crashing waves, here I felt so free*
*the woman I met here unlocked the door of my heart with her key.*

*Laying out by the pool on my second day, I decided to go for a run*
*seashells covered the sandy shore and people laid out under the sun*
*that's when I saw her, one look and it was my heart she had won.*

*Our eyes met, and I couldn't take mine off of you*
*you couldn't either, as we became engaged in each other's view*
*focusing back forward, my interest in you from then on only grew.*

*Turning back around, still you stared at me and then smiled*
*inside I got that excited feeling, as if I were a little child*
*you seemed like a faithful woman, not my past ones who were wild.*

*Stars shining high in the sky, that night I dreamt of you in bed*
*only seeing you once, yet I couldn't get you out of my head*
*if I didn't see you again, my heart would bleed out and be dead.*

*T*he next day I walked the sandy beach and I was bound
to see you, but when I searched you were nowhere to be found
sadly turning around, I walked back with my head to the ground.

*M*aking my way up the sandy slope, I lifted my head and behold
there you were, waiting for me, your smile more precious than gold
walking up to you, I was excited to see what was next to unfold.

*A*fter exchanging names and small talk, down to the sea we went
music playing somewhere, we took in the salty ocean scent
seeing a ring on your finger, meeting you I'm starting to resent.

*Y*ou say, "I'm not married. It's to keep other guys away"
I smile happily, glad that we can continue on with our day
looking at you, you shine brighter than any single sun ray.

*D*inner over candlelight and drinking the reddest of wine
are we meant to be together? Was today some kind of sign?
all I could think about is that I wanted to make you all mine.

*R*emoving our shoes and holding hands, the ocean wets our feet
something romantic is happening here, can you feel the heat?
stopping me, our lips connect, and yours taste heavenly sweet.

*S*hould we slow things down? Are we going too fast?
I feel like we've known each other, as if best friends from the past
heart exploding within my chest, I have found true love at last.

*W*alking you home, like a gentleman I take my leave at the door
beliefs we share, but it's hard to not go inside and do so much more
one last look for the night, you're so beautiful in the dress you wore.

*Two days pass, and my stay in the OBX is coming to its close*
*sadly vacations end, unfortunately that's just how it goes*
*after I leave, when will we meet again? Only God above knows.*

*My last day arrives, and inside I'm filled with sorrow*
*an amazing week spent with you, I'm not ready to leave tomorrow*
*we've grown like husband and wife, it's time I wish I could borrow.*

*One last romantic dinner for two, inside my heart is hurt*
*not wanting to leave you, you look gorgeous in your maxi skirt*
*clinging to my side, we laugh, kiss, and feed each other dessert.*

*Near the ocean we lay, talk, and stay up most of the night*
*enjoying one another, making out, above the moon shines bright*
*we want to go so much further, it's the temptation we must fight.*

*Dawn breaks, and the hardest thing to do is leaving you*
*bags packed and plane ticket in hand, I'm feeling down and blue*
*kissing me you say, "Cheer up, one day we'll be together soon!"*

*My spirit up after you say this, now there is no need to mope*
*with this good news bringing me joy, now I'm able to cope*
*I pray we reunite sooner than later, this I can only hope.*

*Holding you tightly one last time, I look up at the clock*
*French kissing you many times, I let you go and start to walk*
*on the airplane thinking of you, without you I'm still in shock.*

*Life alone back at home, inside my head all I see is your name*
*a summer beach romance filled with love, baby I miss our flame*
*we talk on the phone, but not seeing you just isn't the same.*

*My* burning to see you grows, I have to see you soon, like now
*it's better not to make promises, but to you I'm making this vow*
*"one day we'll be together soon," is gonna happen quickly somehow.*

*A* card arrives in the mail from you, I open it as I lay
*surprising me you write, "OBX in a week, what do you say?"*
*smiling I say to myself, "don't worry baby, I'll be on my way!"*

*3/26/2017*

*There's something about the ocean and its stunning features that broadcasts the word magical and welcomes the romantics. Waves crashing, footprints in the sand, the ever-inviting sounds it offers...the watery world and its atmosphere most certainly comforts the heart and makes one feel right at home, even if it's miles away from the actual one you live in. With visiting this majestic realm many times in my life, I look forward to the day to be there once again.*

# *The Other Poems*

*Firefighter Rastin Challenge, 2016. In case you've never experienced this 224 step (14 stories) monster, it's a challenging tower to climb, especially in full turnout gear and bottle! Our team got 1st, and, not boasting, I ran the quickest time. 59 seconds to be exact.*

# Broken Hearted

*This poem started it all for me. Back in high school, I entered Broken Hearted into a competition out of state and the organization wanted to put it into a book. However, due to reasons I'm not going to explain, I chose to keep it out of it. But now here it is, in an actual book! We all suffer through broken hearts at times and for various reasons. Broken hearts paralyze us, make us feel empty, shatter our lives for a time; but, with time and support, broken hearts can be mended back together.*

# Broken Hearted

Confused and paralyzed I feel broken
but you don't care as I stand in the open.
I feel crumbled, it seems like I'm blinded
yet it really doesn't matter because you don't mind it.
You're driving me crazy, I'm going to burst
can your hatred possibly get any worse?
You've got me feeling like I'm trapped in a maze
but I will stand firm getting through your reckless ways.
To you I'm just a shadow in the dark
a fire ready to blaze but without a spark.
I'm disgusted by your thoughtless and corrupted mind
searching for your kindness which I can't seem to find.
You walk past me as if I was invisible
saddened because you're making me miserable.
I thought you were a friend but are really a fool
why are you like this weighing down my soul?
I'll never give in to your false and unjust action
keep from me, I can't stand you with a passion.
Do whatever you want, you won't break me apart
forever I will have my true and loving heart.

8/28/2005

# My Place

*One of my personal favorite poems, My Place goes out to my parents, Dave and Renee, my brother Nick, and to all my friends who considered My Place home. Thank you all for hilarious, crazy, and fun-filled memories that I'll never forget. My parents' house was the place to be for us growing up, and no matter what we got into, my parents were loving enough to put up with us. Mama and Pops, thank you, and I'll never understand what all you went through and did for us "knuckleheads!" The poem says it all, but some things were omitted!*

# My Place

*R*unning up and down the neighborhood, my heart would race

*playing basketball till 2 A.M., bending down to tie my shoelace*
*looking back, we were loud, like right up in your face*
*rewind with me to my youth, where we lived at my place.*


*B*ack in high school, my house was the place to be

*"mooning" cars at the top of the street, afterward we would flee!*
*Our crew consisted of boys just looking to have some fun*
*reminiscing, I can't believe all the things that we had done.*
*To my friends, my place was like their second home*
*always welcome, at my place nobody was to be on their own.*
*Never missing America's Funniest Home Videos, we would laugh*
*all the things we used to do, trust me, you don't wanna know the half.*
*Always on the menu was the famous stromboli from Dirko's*
*when it came to keeping the neighborhood up, boy we were pros.*
*When "mooning" turned into egging and paintballing cars, I didn't have a hand*
*even though I still stood with the crowd, all I could think was getting sent to the can!*
*To my neighbors and to the victims of all of our rowdy ways*
*I pray you forgive me for my adolescent and rebellious days.*
*Not caring about other traffic as we rode dirt bikes up and down the street*
*Mama making breakfast for us idiots in the morning was quite the treat.*
*Driving the golf cart all around, I can't believe it never died*
*memories never to be forgotten, I hold them always deep inside.*
*We thought we were real tough, smoking Black and Milds by the packs*
*we may have done a lot of dumb things, but at least we had each other's backs.*
*Staying up all night, laughing our heads off, and never falling asleep*
*our conversations I'll always treasure, some shallow, but many of them deep.*
*Remember Yahoo Messenger and the crushes we had on girls?*
*late night toilet papering, in the sky the stars shined like pearls.*
*Alcohol, drugs, and sex to us was nothing but a waste of time*
*who needed that stuff when we formed our own kind of high!*
*Even though we were wild and free, we could also be very sweet*
*messes we would make, but in the morning we had everything looking neat.*

*If Pops knew of some of the things I did, he would've surely wrung my neck*
*BB gun wars, I'll never forget my brother leaving my face a wreck.*
*Hey Max! How about a game in my bedroom of NFL Blitz?*
*you never could beat me, time to put your controller down and call it quits!*
*Playing cards, our money back then was substituted to betting fireworks*
*meals, a roof, clothing, and a heck of a time, staying at my place had its perks.*
*Laughing and shaking my head, at my place we had so many great times*
*even though we sound bad, look at our records, none of us have any crimes!*
*To my family and my old squad, I say this from the heart*
*thank you for all the memories and times, from within they will never depart.*
*Reader: thanks for traveling back with me and entering my youth*
*like a flower, this was me at one time, it's a part of my roots.*

*E*ven though we were young and sometimes lacked a brain

*we could bring the sunshine, and at other times make it rain*
*down the hill is where you can find us, at my place we'll always reign*
*long live the boys who brought noise and caused raucous on Heritage Lane!*

*3/3/2017*

*This was the real deal right here. My friends and I at My Place. Sorry you're not in the picture Craig, but you showed up later that night for another one. Not sure what year this was, it sure does take me on a stroll down memory lane. I always let my little brother Nick hangout with the big boys - he was one of us - and I had his back no matter what. That's him below us happily holding Gretchen, our family pet dachshund growing up.*

# The Firefighter

*The Firefighter was written before I ever became a fireman, but since my sophomore year of high school, I knew this was the profession for me. I love my job (Firefighter/Paramedic) and what I do, and I'm humbly honored to share in an occupation where many have served and perished attempting to save others. As a Firefighter, we are all created equal by God, and we firemen aren't scared to enter where many would never venture into.*

# The Firefighter

When there is a fire and the people are about
don't worry, the firefighter is there to put it out.
Ready for whatever dressed in his gear
the firefighter is heroic and has no fear.
When he hears the call he is ready
he's never nervous but stays steady.
Running to the firefighting truck he is brave
going to stop the fire even if he's sent to his grave.
He is confident as he risks his life
going to save people: children, husband, and wife.
The fireman is always on duty and does his best
he loves doing his job and doesn't give it a rest.
Always giving up his life to save others
as he works with his friendly band of brothers.
The dependable firefighter is always someone you can count on
he will never stop fighting until that blazing fire is gone.
The fireman is a hard working, courageous man
no matter the problem he will lend a helping hand.

8/29/2005

# Why The Hate ?

*There are many signs, events, and things that go on in our world that sadly partner with hate. Why The Hate ? was written to show and boldly state that there's an opposing side that stands for so much more, and is so much better. With writing, I'm always going to be positive, light up darkness, and point toward love. There are two sides: love and hate. I'm standing with love.*

# Why The Hate *?*

*T*oday's world is so full of hate
it brings so much fate
and it's so hard for it to escape.

*I*nstead of this let's treat and be kind to each other

let's erase the hate and do our best to recover.
Because until the end we will all be together
let us take away the pain and change our ways forever.
Be happy and keep righteousness in your mind
always being good to one another by being kind.
We must love and care for one another
and start looking at each other as if we are sister and brother.
If things go wrong, let us not set apart
search deep and do what is right in your heart.

*T*ogether let's do the best that we can do

let us keep the old way but also make it new
forever let's cherish and love each other too.

*8/31/2005*

# Dear God

*Dear God is my letter of thanksgiving to God for Who He is and what He's done for me in my life. I am a Christian - I say this with joy - but that doesn't make me superior or better than a single person, and I've never acted this way toward a single soul. I make mistakes, I've sinned many times, and I'm still being perfected daily, but my hope is in something so much greater than what this world believes or offers - in God, and His Son Jesus Christ and His resurrection. You will never find me shoving God or Jesus down anyone's throat - that's a personal decision that one must make if they choose to - but I will live as an example to highlight God's grace that has been extended to me and is available to all. That includes you, reader!*

# Dear God

*F*ather, which art in Heaven high above

*thank You for my life and Your compassionate love.*
*With You in my life I'm truly bound to win*
*living this life doing my best to stay away from sin,*
*by showing love to others and by always believing*
*in this world I shall not blaspheme or be deceiving.*
*I shall judge not, for that is not my mission*
*with open ears I shall continue to listen,*
*to the powerful words You speak which are just*
*and to make it to Heaven I will do what I must.*
*Always having faith, Your commandments I will surely keep*
*grateful for our relationship together that runs deep.*
*In this world of evil I fear nothing but You*
*I shall endure to the end by purely being true.*
*Whether my death be by old age or by the sword*
*just know that I live entirely and endlessly for You Lord.*
*Thank You for the many blessings and for this life*
*which at times can be trying, full of hypocrites and strife.*
*But I shall stand for the Son of Man's sake*
*and for the strong sacrifice which He chose to make.*
*Like He, I will strive to be just and forgiving*
*for You are the God not of the dead but of the living.*
*I shall do my best, I may make many a mistake*
*but my righteousness and pure heart no man can break.*
*Living this life for You, I will stay clear of the power of hate*
*for I want to be as a small child entering into Heaven's gate.*
*Hard to anger, loving, and giving I shall always be*
*know God that I believe in and that I only worship Thee.*

*Believing that I'm going to Heaven every night as I pray*
*I shall always love You and Your Son throughout each and every day.*
*As the seasons grow old and the years come anew*
*with all of my heart and soul, God I love You!*

*5/25/2007*

*My mother, Renee, has been a solid foundation in my life. The most blessed of all mothers (to me), a wise counselor, a loving mother/friend...the list goes on. I'll say what's in the hearts of many sons toward their mothers: I wouldn't have gotten far in life without her. A grateful, appreciative, and thankful son, the love between a true mother and son cannot be measured nor contained in mere words. I love you Mother, and thank you!*

# Gretchen

Many of us have pets. I'm a huge pet lover.
Gretchen was a childhood dog - a Dachshund - who
I absolutely loved growing up with. I'll never forget
the day when Pops and I went into the vet to have
her put down - Gretchen had heart complications.
My heart was broken, as I'm sure many of yours
have been from putting down your own animals. In
my Bible study, I have yet to find a definitive
answer as to whether we will see our pets again or
not. I say this because I wrote this poem when I
was younger and based some things on what the
world says. I'm not going to play God, so I leave
you with this: if we do see them again, then we will
rejoice and be glad; if pets are only for us on earth,
then let's enjoy all of our moments with them.

# Gretchen

*I* miss my baby dog Gretchen

loving her by giving her much attention.
She was such a good dog
and O how she ate like a hog.
But you see now she's gone
and I've mourned for her so long.
Missing her twenty-four-seven
don't have to worry because all dogs go to Heaven.
She was so playful and kind
for she will always be stuck in my mind.
Boy do I miss her, yes
she always thought she was a little princess.
When she died a piece of me went away
but I know I'll see her again someday.
I'll never forget the day she died
how she would always cling to my side.
Now she is in a better place
I will never ever forget her puppy face.
It was funny when she'd tear her toys apart
she forever and always will be in my heart.
She hated to be left alone
would make her happy by bringing home a bone.
Gretchen was like a beautiful pearl
she will always be my baby dog girl.
Walking through the front door with the mail
she'd be sitting there wagging her tail.
I'm going to miss Gretchen so much
how I miss her loveable touch.
I wish that she could've been with me forever
but again, I believe one day we'll be together.

*8/27/2005*

# Forever I Will Be

*The title of this book, it was important to me to find a title that stood for who I am. I felt Forever I Will Be was the perfect fit. I'll always be many things: loving, generous, strong, a firefighter/paramedic, author, woodworker, hardworking, dependable, trustworthy…etc. I'm not boasting of these characteristics or achievements, but this is who I am and I'm not going to change. For two reasons: 1) because God loves me just the way I am - living for and glorifying Him - and 2) people love and respect me based on living for God, whether they acknowledge that or not. I have love for all people, regardless of their past, color, nationality, upbringing, etc., and that love includes you! This is how Forever I Will Be.*

# Forever I Will Be

*P*eople who know me know that I care
*when they're down and sad I'm always there*
*I'm big but everybody knows I'm a loveable teddy bear.*

*T*hroughout my life I've set a great plan
*part of it is that I fear no man*
*when you're in need I'll lend a helping hand.*

*L*ike I said I fear no man, whatever the size
*I'll never give up but will always go for the prize*
*I'm gonna love and cherish my life until it's my demise.*

*N*o matter the challenge I will give it my all
*you can try to bring me down but I'll always stand tall*
*push and beat me but I will never fall.*

*T*ry to confuse me but I'm too smart
*I'll never change, I have too big of a heart*
*I know I'll make it in life, nothing will break me apart.*

*W*hen trouble comes I don't look for a fight
*to God I pray to watch over me and my loved ones every night*
*for the rest of my life I'm gonna do what is just and right.*

*G*oing to be helpful to my friends, sticking up for one another

till the day I die I'm gonna love my younger brother
always taught to be nice and have manners from my wonderful mother.

*I*f ever you feel like you're in denial

give me a call, all you gotta do is dial
you can always find me wearing my happy, loving smile.

*T*his is the way I am, I hope you can see

if you're ever in need you can always count on me
until the day I die this is how forever I will be.

8/28/2005

*Me being my amusing self – once you get to know me a little – I'm a devoted and loyal fan of the Teenage Mutant Ninja Turtles. Since childhood I've always been a fan, and always will be. Though it can't be seen, this shirt has a cape on the backend that waves in the wind when moving faster than a walk. The eye mask is red, representing my favorite TMNT of all: Raphael, the one with attitude!*

# Christmas Feeling

*A holiday poem I had a lot of fun writing, Christmas Feeling puts you right in the Christmas mood. There's something about this season that seems more giving, merry, caring, and loving. It's too bad we don't treat every day and everybody as if it were this time of year. We all have our own Christmas traditions, feelings, and ways of doing things. I wanted to share some of mine with you. To me the ending of this poem sums up what CHRISTmas is truly all about. Merry Christmas to you all!*

# *C*hristmas *F*eeling

*S*now's falling from the sky
*mistletoes are hung on high*
*children, the time to open your presents is nigh.*

*T*ime to pop in those favorite movies like Home Alone
*dress snugly, or that winter wind will chill you to the bone*
*Christmastime isn't the time to be on your own.*

*T*he tree is decorated, shining brightly like a star
*counting down to Christmas morning, the day isn't far*
*Little Cindy's wish list: a doll, a sled, and a future sports car!*

*O*utside, the children play in the snow
*candlelight's in windows shine their warm glow*
*Santa on his sleigh bellows Ho! Ho! Ho!*

*P*resents are wrapped, hot chocolate's steaming, and the Christmas songs are blaring
*tis the season of miracles, where people's spirits seem more caring*
*it's more blessed to give than to receive, so don't forget the importance of sharing.*

*P*eople caroling on sidewalks and the city is filled with joy
*Santa's elves have been busy making toys for every girl and boy*
*rockin' around the Christmas tree is no other than Uncle Roy.*

*C*ookies are cut out and iced, the punch is just right, and the supper table looks yummy
*a popular time for the common cold, so pack Kleenex for that nose that's runny*
*open your heart and wallet for the hungry who have a rumbling in their tummy.*

$S$led riding under the brilliance of the bright, pale moon

get to bed little ones, Santa's coming very soon
Last Christmas, Jingle Bell Rock, The Chipmunk Song - what's your favorite Christmas tune?


$W$ho knows how to explain it, but there's something about that Christmas feeling

something uplifting, magical, and to the heart brings healing
that sends our thoughts soaring high, even above the ceiling.


$T$rying not to forget about anyone, shopping at the mall

for goodness sake, be careful of the ice, you wouldn't want to fall
Christmas means so much, but what I'm about to tell you is the most important of it all:


$A$ Savior named Immanuel was born, wrapped in cloths and lying in a manger

to those who believe He is the Lord, but to others He is only a stranger
do not be afraid to welcome Him into your heart, there is no danger.


$H$is name is Jesus, and the essence of Christmas is found only in Him

sad because many during this time want His light to become dim
taking Him out of the true meaning of this season, but those chances are slim.


$C$hurch bells chime and hymns are sung, remembering on this night

the birth of God's Son, and with Him came light
Whose love is for all, igniting our spirit, and lifting us to a graceful height.


$S$o bow your head, give thanks, and let us celebrate so the world will see

where our joy comes from, that it is found only in He
to all a good and blessed night as I pray on both of my knees.


*11/17/2016*

*Out in wonderful Canada on a fishing trip, summer 2013. With a huge walleye in my hand, no fishing compares to that of Canada. I've been going there on fishing trips with my Pops for years, and it's so peaceful and soothing - no cell service or electronics, and you're miles away from any human life!*

# I Miss Your Soul

*Ever have a friend who seemed to change just over night? Someone who was close, but all too quickly took a turn down a different path? I Miss Your Soul is for those people who have experienced this hardship. There have been some people in my life who I thought I knew, but the longer I was around them, the more their true colors showed, and I had no clue who they were anymore. A true friend sticks closer than a brother. Hopefully you have at least one of them in your life. If you have more, I say you're blessed.*

# I Miss Your Soul

*I* don't know what's happened to you these past days
but you've got me damaged and imprisoned in a maze.
Trying to perceive through your eyes to look deep down inside
searching for that precious soul of yours that must have died.
You've changed to the point where I don't understand
your hateful and pitiful behavior is out of this land.
Thought I caught a glimpse but you're really gone
haven't felt your friendship for a while, it's been long.
Try to reach for you but I'm blocked off by your conflicting bars
it's going to take a while but I know that time will heal my scars.
It takes time but you've got me feeling broken down
below the earth's surface, deep into the ground.
I didn't think it could happen but you broke my heart
it's like you snatched it from my chest and shattered it apart.
You used to be compassionate and friendly but now act a fool
why can't you change to your old self? I miss your soul.

9/5/2005

# Give It Your All

*Though a short poem, Give It Your All is also a strong and encouraging poem. I, for one, definitely wished I would've tried harder in certain things during my youth. Take sports for instance. Now, mature and older, I give my all in all I do. My Grandma Arck bought me an inspirational plaque a long time ago that I keep hung on my weight room wall so I can always see it. It says: What Would You Do If You Knew You Could Not Fail? Is that encouragement or what? Don't be afraid. Go out and give things your all!*

# Give It Your All

*Throughout life comes many a test*
*don't be afraid, instead give it your best*
*keep practicing and trying, don't give it a rest.*

*Go out and keep on fighting*
*don't ever give up or stop trying*
*if it doesn't go your way, don't be crying.*

*Instead, do your thing and give it your all*
*get yourself back up if you fall*
*never stop believing, always stand tall.*

*8/31/2005*

# The Special Individual

*There are people who show up in our lives who impact us in ways that many others don't. They don't come around that often, but when they do, we sure are happy they did. Someone who is positive, trustworthy, a joy to talk to, who looks at the world and its circumstances differently, and who you enjoy seeing and being around. In regards to The Special Individual, be thankful for these individuals and make every encounter with them as if it is your last. Because you just never know, one day they may no longer be around.*

# The Special Individual

*D*id you hear about the new kid who came to town?
*from California to Ohio, he's been all around.*
*He strives to be the best, his beliefs not to be blended*
*honesty and fairness is what he recommended.*
*Each and every day he takes a chance*
*people want to see him, even if it's only a glance.*
*He has seen the world through his eyes*
*he never quits, but confidently goes for the prize.*
*Throughout his life he has done his best*
*always does he look for the answer, doesn't like to guess.*
*As he gets older he knows circumstances will arise*
*he will stand up to the challenge, no matter the size.*
*Although the grass decays and the flower becomes deceased*
*he keeps his head high, knowing he lived his life in peace.*
*Did you hear about the new kid who came to town?*
*people are sad and miss that he is no longer around.*

*2002 or 2003*

# Martyrs

*I purchased a book sometime back called Foxe's Book of Martyrs, a famous book telling of the lives, persecutions, and victorious deaths of Christians who have died for their faith, dating back from the very first martyrs to the now present ones. This book definitely opened up my eyes to this world, how it once was, and how it currently is. I felt strongly compelled to dedicate a poem to those who have given their life for the Gospel. To those who don't believe the Christian faith, these deaths may seem a waste. But to those who believe, their death is swallowed up in victory!*

# Martyrs

*Long, long ago, there were brave men and women who stood strong for their belief*
*who were treated awfully and with contempt, and many of their lives were brief.*

*Though death tightened its grip on them, still their faith was solid as a rock*
*refusing to deny their Lord, it was the Kingdom of Heaven one day they would walk.*

*Their blood screams as a testimony, and through my studies I have found*
*no one could rob them of their joy, even when their accusers tried to bury their name in the ground.*

*These Christian brothers and sisters may have died, but one day they will rise*
*they are to be remembered, so to you I will speak of their demise.*

*The first martyr, Stephen, of The New Testament, spoke with the Spirit in his breath*
*but the leaders of his day dragged him away, and stoned him to his death.*

*What about Peter? Jesus' disciple who denied Him, repented, and didn't die by the sword*
*instead, he was crucified upside down, because he didn't feel worthy to die as his Lord.*

*Enter the Roman era: believers were fed to lions, broiled over fire, and with hooks their flesh was torn*
*others were beheaded, had their brains bashed out with clubs, and were treated with the highest of scorn.*

*Now the Inquisition years: men of faith like John Huss and many more were burned alive at the stake*
*George Wishart forgave his executioner before he died, how do you explain love like this that no man can shake.*

*Translating the Bible into English, William Tyndale, a simple and trusting man, to his death was strangled*
*while John Hooper prayed while burning, and yet other followers of The Way were mangled.*

*Others throughout history were buried alive like Vitalus, while others were tarred and set on fire*
*so many Christians clung to their faith and beliefs, even when their life came down to the wire.*

*Present day: radical extremists are setting off bombs, hacking people to death, and severing their head*
*killing many others in various ways and without mercy, it's inhuman what I have read.*

*I could go on and on, but the number of Christians martyred for their faith is far too much*
*remember them I will – their lives, boldness, and courage – it is my heart that they touch.*

*Place your feet in their shoes. What would you have done with a martyr's death staring you in the face?*
*would you have boldly clung to your faith if instead you were put in their place?*

*If you're a believer or if you're not, I just wanted you to see*
*how many Christians were, have been, and are treated – people like you and me.*

*Now, most people wouldn't be willing to die for their beliefs, so straight up here's the truth*
*what Christians have died for is not a waste because the Lord is real, and their deaths are living proof.*

*People aren't willing to die for something that is made up or false, wouldn't you agree?*
*so you see, these men and women died for what is certain, that which sets you free.*

*Overcome with emotion, if I had lived back then, what would I have done?*
*died for my faith I like to believe, not turn my back on the Lord and run.*

*As I think of all the past, present, and future Christian martyrs, I feel it in my heart*
*to follow their example, live for the Lord, die if I must, and for God always live my part.*

*5/16/2017*

*On a mission trip in Haiti, 2014. This was one of many of my little buddies I met, and his name is Jimmy. He was super excited when I gave him my Teenage Mutant Ninja Turtles book bag on our last day! You can't tell by his face, can you!?*

# First Day Of School

*Specifically speaking, I remember my very first day of high school as a freshman and the apprehensiveness I felt within. Was I going to get picked on? Would the upperclassmen bully me in sports? Did a swirly in the boy's bathroom await me? The first day ended up going by very well, and gradually I fitted right in as time passed. What about you? Do you remember your first thoughts before ever stepping into new territory and your first day of school? With First Day Of School, I wanted to bring back to mind the thoughts, feelings, fears, uncertainties, and the expectations back to memory. Looking back, it really wasn't so bad, was it?*

# First Day Of School

*T*oday is the first day of school
*it's a bunch of bull.*
*It's bad because my class is the youngest*
*but I'm going to try and make this year the funnest.*
*This year I'm just praying that I pass*
*as I take my first step into class.*
*Wishing it was time to be picked up by my dad*
*but this day isn't actually going by so bad.*
*Third period is accomplished*
*can't wait till this day is over, I wished.*
*Wondering how long this day will last*
*as the day starts to go by fast.*
*Now I'm headed to lunch*
*getting my papers in a bunch.*
*Playing dodge ball in gym has been fun*
*knowing that this day is almost done.*
*In History I learned how to form an alliance*
*now I'm headed to my last period which is Science.*
*Science has always made me throw a fit*
*but I'm going to do my best to get through it.*
*The bell rings for school to end*
*I say, "See ya," to my best friend.*

*This first day didn't bring any fate*
*because it was honestly really great.*
*My first day of school didn't bring any sorrow*
*matter of fact, I can't wait to come back tomorrow.*

*2002 or 2003*

*One of my young elementary school pictures, I believe 2nd grade. I've been truly blessed in life, experiencing so much: family, friends, mission trips serving people, being an author-firefighter-paramedic-woodworker…sports, vacations, good and hard times, and so much more. I could die today a very blessed, happy man!*

# Goodbyes

*We humans - many times - think of the word
"goodbye" as something ending or a length of time
being separated. A friend going away for a long
time, a spouse taking leave at an airport for
business, someone saying it before they die, a
family member going on a mission trip, etc. There's
a nameless uneasiness about the word and the
feeling it leaves inside. But the word "goodbye"
also brings to life the hope of seeing again someday,
being together soon, and the comfort that the time
to rejoin approaches. I hope you feel something
positive in your spirit after reading Goodbyes.*

# Goodbyes

No one enjoys when it comes down to goodbyes
it seems to invite sad faces with tearful eyes.
Leaving a loved one or friend isn't easy
causes people to feel lonesome and queasy.
That last hug or kiss will forever be treasured
the likeness or love is strong, and cannot be measured.
Goodbyes allow the realization of coming together again one day
it may seem long but it will come in an unexpected, beautiful way.
Reliving that final glance as it remains always inside the head
remembering the ending conversation of what was last said.
There's always a will and way to rejoin again in time
nobody knows when but it comes somewhere down the line.
Look at goodbyes as if you found something valuable that was lost
but reclaim it again and keep it forever, no matter the cost.

9/2/2005

# Poems

With writing Poetry, I felt I needed to devote a poem toward it. I was never a huge fan of Poetry, but as soon as I started reading some rhyming poems, I soon became Poetry's biggest fan! Maybe it's just me, but something clicks in us humans when writing and rhyming combine together. Whether it is a story, a song, a poem, etc., we look forward to what word is going to be rhymed next. I write poems of all genres, and I love being able to tell short stories from different emotions and perspectives. Like my fiction novels, I'm going to continue writing poems until the ideas stop coming or I get tired of them. P.S., I'm hoping neither ever happens!

# *Poems*

*I* write poems because they take me to a place <u>only I know</u>
a place where I can <u>go alone</u> to let the <u>words just flow</u>.
I compose <u>love poems</u> for <u>the lovers</u> who found someone in life
who have <u>searched to find</u> the absolute perfect husband or wife.
I devise <u>sad poems</u> for people who have had a <u>broken heart</u>
but <u>find a path</u> that is brighter for <u>a better start</u>.
I formulate <u>happy poems</u> for good will and <u>sunny days</u>
<u>smiles and laughter</u> that set forth for <u>higher ways</u>.
I write poems that people will <u>truly love</u> and greatly enjoy
reminiscing about the <u>good years</u> when they were a younger girl or boy.
I <u>envision poems</u> because I know <u>what people feel</u> deep down inside
feelings <u>nobody else understands</u> that they prefer to hide.
I create poems in <u>remembrance of someone</u> you have feelings for
who you think of <u>all the time</u> and could never possibly ever ignore.
I write poems so others can read them all <u>around the earth</u>
cherishing my writings and how much they are <u>worth</u>.
<u>Not worth as of money</u>, but worth as special and with belief
my poems come <u>from the heart</u> with joy and <u>without any grief</u>.
I write poems so that a <u>smile</u> will come across your face
hoping that my poems are <u>heartfelt</u> and make for <u>a lovely place</u>.

8/22/2005

# Nothing Lasts Forever

*The reality of this poem, Nothing Lasts Forever, can be a pang to our hearts. The houses we live in, the jobs we work, the youth we try to hold on to for as long as we can, the talents and skills, our families and friends, our present lives - I could go on and on, but you're getting my point - none of it is going to last and one day it will all be gone. We start out young thinking we're invincible and that we're guaranteed an old age. We live life from the perspective that tomorrow is always going to come and that we're going to be there with it. I live life knowing that a year isn't promised, tomorrow isn't promised, heck, I even live my life knowing that this very day isn't promised. I'm not attempting to scare anyone with Nothing Lasts Forever, but it's time to start living our lives like today is the last day we have by loving and being kind to others, getting our hearts right, being thankful, and living life from the mindset that Nothing Lasts Forever.*

# Nothing Lasts Forever

*Everyone please be thankful and love living your life*
*men, cherish every second you spend with your wife.*
*Enjoy the places you go and people you meet*
*appreciate the sunny weather even if it's too much heat.*
*Be grateful for vacations and beautiful places*
*as well as each and every one of God's graces.*
*Always be fortunate to be able to live free*
*and for all the fabulous things that you see.*
*Having fun playing sports and doing things you're talented in*
*always be thankful for all of your friends and kin.*
*It's not about money or the fancy cars*
*or having a good time drinking at the bars.*
*You're going to make mistakes but stay smart*
*abandon the ways of man and search deep in your heart.*
*In the end who cares about all this stuff*
*just do your best and always be tough.*
*Cherish everything that means anything to you*
*even though it's not everlasting let it remain true.*
*Be thankful for sunny days and beautiful weather*
*for it is said in the end that nothing lasts forever.*

*9/4/2005*

# For The Women

*Like most teenage boys and young men, I too was once crazy about girls/women. Never a "womanizer" or trying to get with as many as I could, I instead was always the serious relationship type and was always for one woman. For The Women was my way of announcing that this is who I am and this is what I offer, thinking that this is what any reasonable woman would want out of a man.*

# For The Women

*A*ttention all women scattered throughout this land

*if you're looking for someone faithful I'm your man.*
*Men that don't treat women right have some nerve*
*many ladies are ignored and get what they don't deserve.*
*Not bragging by any means but I'm loving and kind*
*I'm here for you if you're looking for someone to find.*
*Giving you all the affection and pleased to mention*
*that I will give you all of my love and attention.*
*Surely I'll always be honest, trustworthy, understanding*
*I promise I'll offer nothing but happiness, never demanding.*
*Bringing smiles and laughter upon your face will be a warming sight*
*filling your life with love, I will forever care and hold you tight.*
*I'm not moody, you won't have to worry about me being in a bad mood*
*communication we will have, I'll not ever be impolite or rude.*
*Showing the world that I cherish being with you*
*it's hard for many to do but I will always be true.*
*Hope all you women accept the way I am*
*in case I forgot to inform you my name is Jared McCann.*

*8/25/2005*

119

# Thankful

*I'm going to be real honest here. Most days I hear people complain, them never being satisfied, and not being content with what they have. Everything's just mediocre, "okay," or blah to them. If it's one thing I've always been, it's Thankful! I don't drive a high-priced vehicle, I don't live in a mansion, and my bank account isn't anything to brag about; but still I'm appreciative with what I possess and the fact that I have our basic human needs met: food/water on the table, clothes on my back, and a roof over my head. Short and sweet: I'm blessed, content, and Thankful! From going on mission trips, I've seen a lot and I've seen people who don't have much (though they are rich in other areas and have things that I wish I had, and I'm not talking about material possessions). I'm Thankful for everything in my life. I don't take it for granted. I'm not deserving of any of it. But I'm going to share it, serve with it, and always be Thankful for it!*

# Thankful

$T$hroughout my life I've been very thankful

always striving to be an outgoing and kind soul.
Grateful that God gave me my mom and dad
raising me to do right and good, not bad.
Appreciative for my friends and loved ones
they care for me and love me tons.
Thankful for being talented in sports such as baseball
also football when it comes around during the fall.
Blessed for things I get to do and the places I go
when people told me to do bad things I would say "no."
Every night saying my prayers before I go to bed
going to live my life to the fullest until I'm dead.
I'm fortunate for all the people and beautiful places I see
thankful to live in a free and peaceful country.
Thankful for a bunch
so very much.
Thankful for so much more
living and what I stand for.
Thankful for all of God's gifts and every one of His blessings
give thanks in your heart and express it outwardly is what I'm professing.

*2002 or 2003*

# Dry Your Eyes

*All of us go through sad times in our lives. How comforting it is to have a companion at our side. And sometimes words don't even need to be said; their quiet company oftentimes is just the thing we need. Specifically speaking, Dry Your Eyes is about a man being there for his woman when she's down and blue. He doesn't understand why she's in the current state she's in, but he's going to be by her side and try to make it better, even if it's just a little bit. From Solomon in the book of Ecclesiastes: Two people are better off than one, for they can help each other succeed. If one person falls, the other can reach out and help.*

# Dry Your Eyes

*B*aby I can't stand to see you cry
it's making me wonder why?
Is something wrong, why are you so sad
or rather it's something else, are you mad?
Please wipe off your cheeks, I can't stand it
your sadness, I'd do anything to make it quit.
Each time I look at you all I see is tears
did someone die? I'll drive away your fears.
Please stop, I love you too much
let me hold and comfort you with my loving touch.
The tears start to decrease, but only a few
it's all right baby, I'm here for you.
Take it easy and rest
lay your tiresome head on my chest.
We're going to get you through this
would it make things a little better if I gave you a kiss?
I know that you've had a horrible day
but baby please make the tears go away.

*2002 or 2003*

# Life

We all know the popular saying, "Life is short." Growing up as kids, we think Life is long and that the day of adulthood is a century away. But then our adult years arrive and we find that the years start to pass by like the blink of an eye. Our lives are filled with decisions (both good and bad), choices (both wise and poor), consequences, accomplishments, ups and downs, good times and bad, and so much more that's contained in our short lives here on earth. All of us have a past, present, and future; and what we do will have an impact on others when it's our time to leave, whether good or bad. I pray you reflect on your Life and where you're at now. Celebrate it, change it if need be, dig deeper, search for truth, and leave a mark that others will honor. I'm not sure what gave me the inspiration to write this poem back then, but I'm sure glad I did. Using positive words and an encouraging voice, Life is spent so much better with meaning in it and living it right. Because one day it's not going to be here.

# Life

Sometimes life gets hard

it's just a matter of how you play your card.
Not everything goes your way
try to make every morning a bright day
what do you say?
I know sometimes your friends can treat you like crap
go up and tell them, "What is up with that?"
Always hold your head up high
even when people give you a cold sigh
challenge everything, don't be scared to try.
Treat others the way you would want to be treated
instead of being cruel and making yourself feel cheated.
When things don't go your way, don't pout
just stick your chest out
and prove to those people what you're about.
Don't always try to act your coolest
make sure you live your life to the fullest.
Live every day like it's brand-new
just being you
and sticking up for yourself too.
Life will get rough and you'll shed some tears
but stay tough and do what is right through the years.
After this great test
it will be your time to rest
but at least you'll know you lived your life giving it your best.

*2002 or 2003*

# Miscarriage

*The hardship of Miscarriage has affected many women, possibly even yourself. This poem paints an illustration of what may have been if that boy or girl were to have been born. Though we don't have all the answers as humans and we can't comprehend all of life's events, for some reason, whether we like it or not, Miscarriages occur and happen for a reason. To those who have experienced a Miscarriage, I don't have the words for you, nor will I attempt to try and understand your pain. I do know this though: your life does go on and you have a purpose, so keep your head up and shine your smile for all to see. Miscarriage or not, you're beautiful just as you are!*

# Miscarriage

*A* baby girl would've been brought into this world, graceful as ever

*the smile she would've worn and her presence, no one could sever.*
*Would she have been a nurse, or maybe a prom queen?*
*Daddy knows one day she'll fall in love with a king.*
*Her beauty a gift from Heaven, her voice a mellifluous sound*
*Mommy would be there for her when those hard times come around.*
*Knowing she would've shined just as the sun does in May*
*but we will never see, for she was not born on this day.*


*A* baby boy would've been brought into this world, beautiful as ever

*the smile he would've worn and his presence, no one could sever.*
*Would he have been a football player, or maybe a firefighter?*
*having him around would've made Mommy's day a lot brighter.*
*His handsomeness a gift from Heaven, his love was flowing*
*Daddy would be there for him no matter where he was going.*
*Knowing he would've shined just as the sun does over a bay*
*but we will never see, for he was not born on this day.*

*2/3/2007*

# To Be Young

*Remember those days of being young? I sure do, and many of those times I miss, but the past is the past and we now live in our present age. I can recall the mentality of youth: carefree, undisciplined, not always thinking straight, untamed, etc. So many things we take for granted during our youth, and how much we wish we could go back and know then what we know now. What would we have done different? How much more of an effort would we have given? Where would we see ourselves instead? We can ask all day, but one thing is clear: we can't go back and change the past, but we can make efforts today to improve who we are, and how we impact our world and the people around us. I don't know about you, but I still let my youthful self come out and play daily, only now in a more mature, disciplined way.*

# To Be Young

*Many wish they could go back to when they were young*
*doing unwise things, even if they were dumb.*
*To be young means to have fun and to be free*
*toilet papering, but if you see the cops you better flee!*
*Being young means to give everything your best*
*doing things all the time, who needs rest?*
*To be young is doing some of the greatest things in life*
*not to worry about marriage and getting a wife.*
*To be young means dating girls and going to parties*
*back in school doing your best not to get tardies.*
*In junior high always hated to take a test*
*who cares about your bedroom, leave it a mess.*
*Not doing things on time when they need to be done*
*those dog days when all you wanted to do was have fun.*
*To be young means that someday you will get old*
*but I'm gonna enjoy my youth and put those future days on hold.*

*2002 or 2003*

# Bad Day

*Each and every one of us has days that don't quite go the way we would've hoped. A curveball changes the pace of our day, something unexpected comes up and alters our plans, or for some reason a twist keeps us from getting done what we originally wanted to accomplish that day. These days we want to bury our face in a pillow and scream, punch a hole through the wall, and pray as we look forward to a hopeful, better tomorrow. Not every day will go our way, but shrugging off the bad and maintaining a positive attitude will strengthen our character and keep us sane while we're experiencing the difficulties. Rise above life's hard times, because guess what, "this too shall pass."*

# Bad Day

*Wake up late for school*
*God bless my soul.*
*A rainy morning in the middle of May*
*looking in the mirror, I'm going to have a bad hair day.*
*After getting ready I fall down a few stairs*
*but no one's around so who cares.*
*Arrive at school eight on the dot*
*I see someone took my parking spot.*
*Get ripped for being late for class*
*hoping that this day goes by very fast.*
*Stepping into Geometry, I failed my test*
*why won't this day just give me a rest?*
*Praying that this horrible day soon ends*
*wave goodbye as I see a few of my friends.*
*About get in a wreck on the way home*
*today's one of those days I feel stranded alone.*
*Walk into my room*
*happy that this day will be ending soon.*
*As my head hits the pillow I think about this horrible day*
*but now I'm going to sleep and dream it all away.*

*2002 or 2003*

# The Paramedic

*Being a Paramedic, to me, is a lot of words wrapped up in one. You never know what you're going to get into next - which is a very exciting aspect of the job - you see things that a lot of the world doesn't, you're dealing with the life of a human being in your hands, you see a lot of horrible things, most nights you rarely get a good night's sleep, and there are so many other things I could tell you that sum up being a Paramedic. Whether it's pushing medications through an IV line, inserting a tube down someone's trachea, defibrillating someone's heart, or running lights and sirens down a busy street, being a Paramedic is both a rewarding and demanding occupation. Many people are unhappy with their jobs in life; but, I can honestly say, walking through the MVFD's door being a Firefighter/Paramedic on my duty day is something I truly enjoy doing, and every single day.*

# The Paramedic

*W*hen there is a life to be saved in an emergency

*one mustn't worry, the paramedic is responding to the urgency.*
*Whether the patient be a plumber, a businessman, or even a sailor*
*the paramedic will bring a solution to the respiratory failure.*
*The paramedics of this country are here to resuscitate the lives of this nation*
*if one stops breathing, it's time for the honorable paramedic to begin intubation.*
*Whether it's a fracture to be splinted or a wound to be dressed*
*the paramedic will bring back to life the individual who's in cardiac arrest.*
*If for instance one were to break a bone or accidentally be cut with a knife*
*the trustworthy paramedic is there to communicate with and care for your life.*
*Whether the emergency be less critical or a car that wrecked*
*airways, pulse rates, and blood pressures will continually be checked.*
*If trouble breathing, one will receive an efficient non-rebreather mask*
*the paramedic will bring the problem to a successful conclusion whatever the task.*
*When the patient's status appears questionable and the tension gets tighter*
*IVs will be established, medications then given, and the situation made brighter.*
*To parents: whether your child be the eldest, youngest, or the one in the middle*
*the paramedic crew will make a speedy transport to the nearest hospital.*
*In cases of pregnancy when a mother is close to giving birth*
*have faith in the paramedic delivering the neonate for all he or she is worth.*
*Whatever the emergency, keep heart for the paramedic who's on a mission*
*respect this individual and the role of their vital position.*
*Paramedics will bring back the lives of fathers, brothers, sisters, and mothers*
*because paramedics were created to protect and save the lives of others.*

*5/13/2006*

# Key West

*One of my favorite places to vacation, I had to write a poem for that one and only beautiful Key West. Located in Florida, and also boasting the southernmost point of our nation, Key West has a lot of fun things to do and vivid attractions. Snorkeling, sunset sails, fun street walking, tasty food, relaxation - I could go on - Key West offers a lot! I first vacationed in Key West when I was young and I never forgot that trip and how much fun I had there. So much fun that I've been there several times, and I'm planning on going more! If you're wondering where next to go on vacation, trust me, check out Key West. You won't be disappointed!*

# Key West

*On a plane trip to Key West from Ohio*

*Key West is the best place on earth, I know.*
*If I could live any place else it'd be here*
*on a sunny day I'd go fishing on the pier.*
*Laying out tanning in the hot sun*
*visit Key West if you wanna have some fun.*
*Every restaurant here has the finest food*
*in Key West you'll never be in a bad mood.*
*Have the greatest time of your life at Key West*
*no other place beats it, it's the best.*
*Go walking for a good time down Duval Street*
*in Key West many nice people you will meet.*
*Have a fun time in the ocean getting wet*
*or take your "Honey" to see the sun set.*
*Take a romantic walk near the sea*
*you'll never get bored in Key West, I agree.*
*Eat a charming dinner at My Blue Heaven*
*who cares if you don't go to bed, stay up till seven.*
*At Pepe's you can eat a delicious brunch*
*then at B.O.'s you can eat a grouper sandwich for lunch.*
*Key West is a place full of fun and peace*
*from the "real world" it's such a release.*
*If ever you're feeling unhappy and really stressed*
*trust me, go down and take a trip to Key West.*

*12/14/2005*

# Fallen Soldiers

*Remembering our men and women who have served, I most certainly made sure to dedicate a piece of writing to them, back when I wrote this. Every soldier, both deceased and living, means something valuable to someone - they're fathers, mothers, sons, daughters, relatives, and friends - and they mean something to every American citizen because of what they do for us. We all serve in some way, but not all serve in situations that the American soldier does. With this poem, Fallen Soldiers, may we remember what the red, white, and blue flag stands for, celebrate in what that costs, and honor those who serve so that we can have the liberties that we have. To all soldiers, whether dead or living, I personally say, "Thank you."*

# Fallen Soldiers

*Throughout history wars have been going on for years*
*many families and loved ones losing their peers*
*and at the same time shedding tears.*

*Engagements have been going on long before the Civil War*
*listening to the booming of guns with their thunderous roar.*
*To the dead and living soldiers thank you so much*
*for risking your lives for me I owe you a bunch.*
*You brave individuals ventured to keep our country free*
*fighting for your American people, including me.*
*Sad because many won't be coming home for they are deceased and gone*
*but you soldiers died and fought for what was right, not wrong.*
*I can't even imagine all the battles and attacks*
*feel sorry for many because they have flashbacks.*
*War is like a continuing task it seems*
*sad that many of you didn't live to see your dreams.*
*My heart goes out to your families and friends*
*praying that one day all war ends,*
*so things can go back to the good life and be great*
*instead of all this misery and hate.*
*May God watch over you and all your kin*
*for many I'll never grasp how hard your pain has been.*

*It appears endless, a horrible thing that is war*
*it keeps coming every year even more*
*thank you soldiers for being brave and fighting for what the United States*
*stands for.*

*9/2/2005*

# People

*People is definitely one of my most powerful poems. Not holding anything back, I talk about us - People - and how our world currently is, specifically America. How we act, the way things are, and what we're doing, much of it is contained in this poem. I wrote this poem being 29 years of age, and the older I get, the more I see, just as you see more the older you get. I will always love People - and yes, even the difficult ones - but we've got to start making changes and seeing us - People - not as objects, but as People created in the same image who, I pray, will one day respect, build up, strengthen, encourage, and love as if we are all brothers and sisters. This earthly life is short, and it's such a waste to hate, not care for, and block out others and think only of ourselves. It's our lives, and we're going to live them how we want, but I hope we can live them with a deeper appreciation, a more "care for you" perspective, and a stronger love toward us - People.*

# *People*

*A*bundant, different colored, various languages, dissimilar upbringings
some nice, others mean, some crooked, and yet others that shine.
That's right everyone out there, I'm talking about us - people
I have a few things to say, and if you don't agree then that's fine.

*P*ositive by far, I love people but some things I just don't get
like why we won't stand as one - I'm speaking political.
Or how we speak terrible of others but to their faces we're nice
boy, I don't know about you - that seems awfully hypocritical.

*L*ust, drugs, sin, alcohol - in our nation these are an epidemic
too many are forgetting the finer things in life and what is better.
I'm not claiming to be any greater or that I'm without transgression
I too was wrong in many things, but now I'm a forgiven debtor.

*P*utting others down, refusing to help, and turning a cold shoulder
what's wrong with us? Are we blind and no longer care?
If we continue in this downward spiral, not willing to change
I don't like saying it, but we'll be in for one heck of a scare.

*T*he entire family can be happy, but I've found something out
when one member goes astray, it creates quite a storm.
Those individuals don't seem to care about the others' feelings
unfortunately splintered homes instead of peaceful ones have become the norm.

*W*hen holding the door open and letting a vehicle go ahead isn't thanked
it seems the words "Please", "Thank you", and "Excuse me" are forbidden.
Where's the love, the encouragement, the compliments, the respect?
I don't know, but from our hearts it all appears to be hidden.

*M*orality has gone to sleep and most only care about themselves

infidelity, lying, getting ahead by any means, and cursing run rampant.
Certain animals can be tamed, but one thing that isn't is the human tongue
our own mouth too often gets us in trouble - we should learn to clamp it!


*P*rejudiced against others, and I'm not only talking about skin color

have we not learned by now that we're all created in the same image?
How about we share a mutual respect and love for each other
instead of attacking one another on the opposing side of the line of scrimmage.


*A*rrogant comments, cocky attitudes, and pompous egos are bothersome

I got news for you all - God opposes the proud but favors the humble.
In due time those who exalt themselves will themselves be brought low
and the righteous will watch as pride and its followers fall down and crumble.


*I*n a chaotic world filled with ungodliness, all kinds of evil, and ugly

it's enough to make you want to bury your face in a pillow and shout.
Gritting your teeth, slamming your fists, and inner anger are just a few reactions
without a doubt, if you allow it, the world will deliver you a knockout.


*W*ith being who I am, I will finish not in heartache

allow me to conclude positively, filling you with hope.
You're not alone and you need not fear
as if you were wavering toward falling, like walking a tightrope.


*F*aith, love, and grace are real, alive just as you

reach for it, grasp it, and take it in your right hand.
It's freely offered to you, can you not see?
the feeling is grand, like the warmth your toes feel in the sand.


*Y*ou are loved, wanted, you are a masterpiece

be filled with joy, for you shed light just like the sun.
Smile, laugh, and live life with meaning and purpose
run, be one, and know that the victory has already been won.

*B*uild one another up, remember your manners, and show love to all
for your words and actions may have an affect, even if only on one soul.
Stand for what is right, be meek, and don't ever give up
a warning: if you permit it - don't let it - this world will eat you whole.

*I* love people, but some things I will never understand
but I don't need to, because I have peace that reigns within my heart.
If you messed up in life, guess what, we all do, so hang in there
forgiveness is available, and with that a new start.

*M*ay these final words rejuvenate and fill your spirit with comfort
if at this end you disagree with me, that's fine, I'm just trying to promote unity.
We may differ in many ways but I leave you with this:
my prayer is that we all come together, under God, as one community.

12/9/2016

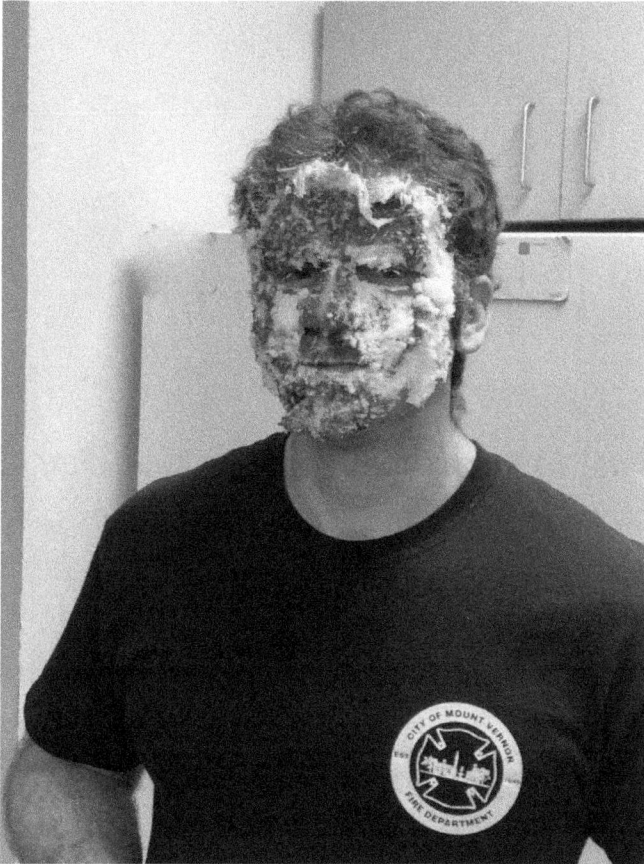

*A personal favorite memory at the firehouse, the guys on my crew – 1 Unit – played a joke on me with a "surprise" cake. Only I got the last laugh, as they weren't expecting me to plunge my face deep into it! It was a raspberry-filled cake, and yes it was delicious, at least for me. The others had to fork around my face print to enjoy whatever remnants they could! Thank you again 1 Unit members!*

# The Best Day

*In contrast to my previous poem, Bad Day, The Best Day is definitely a poem that makes you feel good after reading it. We all have days where everything seems to just be going our way, sometimes even better. These days we need to remember, writing them down or making a mental note even, so that we won't be as upset, disappointed, or mad when we have days that aren't like these ones. I can honestly say I don't ever have a bad day (maybe a tough moment), but I also make a choice and decision to live for a bright day, even in the midst of hard times and the craziness that we experience in our individual lives. Like me, I hope you can celebrate your The Best Days, recall them in your memory, and live trying to make every day like these, even with the not-so-good times that you face in your daily life.*

# The Best Day

*W*ake up feeling refreshed
*brushing my teeth using Crest*
*head to my closet to get dressed*
*feeling great, but I'd be better if only another half hour of rest.*
*Looking into the mirror making sure I look cool*
*starting up my truck to go to school.*
*So far today everything's going my way*
*getting back my Chemistry test, I got an A.*
*In English reading a mystery about the detective Poirot*
*the girl I like asks me what I'm doing tomorrow.*
*I tell her probably hangout, but that I'm ready for the pool this summer*
*then she takes my hand and writes down her phone number.*
*I can't believe what just took place*
*inside my heart is like a race.*
*In the hallway I find a twenty-dollar bill on the floor*
*this day is going my way even more.*
*The bell rings, looking up at the clock, the school day ends*
*say, "Bye, see you tomorrow," to some of my friends.*
*On the way home I blare my music from behind the wheel*
*walking into my house I see my mom made my favorite meal.*
*After eating I'm so very full*
*knowing that I shouldn't have eaten that last roll.*
*Lying on the couch, I realize this day has been so great*
*everything was awesome, especially what I just ate*
*this day brought me all goodness and no hate*
*looking at my hand, I think I'll call the girl I like and ask her on a date.*

*2002 or 2003*

# Death

*This reality - death - is something that touches us all. The passing of a loved one, the death of someone "too young," the life of a friend who is here no longer. One of the toughest deaths to deal with is the death of a child. And then we think to ourselves, "When's it my time?" After all, life is guaranteed to an old age, right? Wrong. We read the newspaper, we see the headlines on TV, we may even deal with it in our jobs, we live in our communities with it - death - and we know one day it's going to be our time. This poem, Death, I didn't write to instill fear or scare, but to start thinking about death a little more compared to not thinking of it at all. Too many people fear death, are scared to "death" of it, and worry about it too much. As a Christian, I have the answer: Jesus Christ! Not pressuring or forcing Jesus on anyone, I say this with love and care for all so that your fears about death will be driven away. It's your decision, but the solution is Jesus, the One who gives life after death.*

# Death

*F*ear, worry, afraid – words like these come to mind

*an emotion of hopelessness, and a sense of feeling blind.*
*This is what many think when they hear the word death*
*not wanting to imagine the day when it's our last breath.*
*Although it's a part of life, it's something we don't often discuss*
*to face this inevitable truth with faith and boldness, we must.*
*A lifeless body, lungs that no longer work, and a heart that stops*
*decayed, stinking, and at rest, we are but a field of dying crops.*
*Loved ones weep, spirits are broken, and friends filled with sorrow*
*life continues as normal, only now you won't be here tomorrow.*
*For others the pain really starts, it's time to attend calling hours*
*lifetime memories surround you, and so do crowds and flowers.*
*In a coffin, though you're "asleep," your family dresses you nice*
*this game we call "life" has ended, you've thrown your last dice.*
*People pay their last respects, and then down you go into the ground*
*six feet under to be exact, and with dirt and dust you are crowned.*
*The grass withers and the flower fades, now no one is no longer here*
*welcome to the cemetery, where there's a forever silence every day of the year.*
*All is gone and stripped from you, like you've become a victim of theft*
*your dwelling place has become the grave, and now there's nothing left.*
*TIMEOUT! WHOA! WAIT A MINUTE! Let Me take over from here*
*death is not the end, and no longer must you live your life in fear.*
*Unlike death I'm alive, and I've defeated death, sin, and even Satan*
*the path of death is crooked, but one day it is all roads I will straighten.*
*Do you want to know the secret to eternal life and how to live free?*
*I am the Way, the Truth, and the Life, and salvation is found only in Me.*
*Those who believe in Me will never die, for they've passed from death into life*
*my Father's Word is alive and powerful, sharper than any sword or knife.*
*Didn't you know I am risen!? My God didn't let Me rot in the grave*
*neither will you if you trust in Me, so don't allow sin to make you a slave.*
*I am coming soon, and it won't be long until I make all things new*
*a resurrection from death and life everlasting, this is what I offer you.*
*Hell is not a place you want to be, for it will tear you to pieces*
*come to Me, all of you who want life after death. My name is Jesus!*

*6/4/2017*

# Where's The Love ?

*We live in a fallen world where hate, corruption, injustice, and sin flourish. Looking out for self, getting ahead by any means, ignoring the needs of others, and lack of compassion is the way of our world. In the midst of all of our world's chaos, there is one thing I continue to see a decrease in: Love. Compliments are scarce, forgiveness is forbidden, hope and faith is for the weak, and the various forms of love seem to have vanished. But this is exactly what our world needs, and what we need to show in our local communities, our state, our nation, our world: Love. "Above all, clothe yourselves with LOVE, which binds us all together in perfect harmony (Colossians 3:14)." Many things can kill, tear down, destroy, and separate, but more powerful than all of these is love. Love will always win!*

# WHERE'S THE LOVE ?

*When tearing down rather than building up has become the
     norm
and instead of sunny skies people choose to be more like a storm
     where's the love?*

*When those overseas are starving, and we refuse to help those in
     our nation's streets
and while we care only for ourselves, putting our feet up and
     leaning back in our seats
     where's the love?*

*When right is now looked at as wrong, and wrong is looked at as
     right
while differences can't be solved, peace has become extinct, and it
     seems there's no hope in sight
     where's the love?*

*While degradation runs rampant, and crime, drugs, and chaos remain
     on the rise, and light appears so far away
when the truth has become twisted, and we look to man for help instead of
     to God who can save the day
     where's the love?*

*When He who knew no sin became sin to die for us lowly human beings on
     a cross
and when we continue to turn away from Him rather than share in His
     glory, resulting in our loss
     where's the love?*

*Instead, why don't we spread our wings like a dove
make a change that sends us flying high toward the sun above
so that we never ask again, "Where's the love?"*

*11/11/2016*

---

149

# Backyard Football

Dedicated to all those who participated, Backyard Football is my shout out to all those who played back in the day at Phillips Park. Whether it was my brother Nick, or high school buddies like John, Craig, Max, Corey, Eric, etc., Backyard Football was something we played a lot back in high school during weekends. Gathering at Phillips Park in the back of the main ball field - before the parking area was put in - most Sundays a lot of us got together, chose two "pickers", and then teams were formed. With no less than 6 on 6, and usually more than that, what followed next was a couple hours' worth of fun, passing, tackling, laughter, and touchdowns! Afterward we'd sit around Phillips Park and talk about all the "highlights" of the games (we usually played more than one). These memories I will always cherish and treasure. To the many of you - you know who you are - who played, I want to personally say, "Thank you for all the memories. May we always remember them with joy in our hearts, and reflect on them often."

# Backyard Football

*Every Sunday me and my boys get together*
*in hot or cold, it doesn't matter about the weather,*
*to play a rough game in which you better not come out lame*
*or you'll get hurt and it will be a shame.*
*Make sure you come out with heart*
*and pray you don't lose a body part.*
*Now the roughhousing begins*
*congratulations to whoever wins.*
*As the quarterback calls the first play*
*I'm hoping that everything goes my team's way.*
*I catch the pass and knock some people around*
*leaving them in the dust, it makes a devastating sound.*
*I love playing this great game of football*
*running into me is like hitting a brick wall.*
*But the game isn't all about pain*
*we have fun, even when it starts to rain.*
*It's about friendship and fun*
*but if you see me you better run!*
*When the game's over, to the benches we walk*
*discussing about what just happened as we talk.*
*Then we call it a day*
*sadly we won't play again until next Sunday.*
*So if you think you're tough, go ahead and come out*
*because my boys and I will show you what we're all about!*

*2002 or 2003*

# Tragedies

*April 20th, 1999. September 11th, 2001. October 2nd - 24th, 2002. October 2nd, 2006. April 15th, 2013. These are the dates of 1) The Columbine High School Massacre, 2) The 9/11 Attacks, 3) The D.C. Sniper Shootings, 4) The West Nickel Mines Amish School Shooting, and 5) The Boston Marathon Bombing. The list goes on in our nation's history, but these were some of the Tragedies that I've lived through and experienced in my lifetime. It's terrible as people what we do to one another, and it's very scary what we human beings are capable of. We've all seen our share of Tragedies in their many forms in each of our lifetimes, and, unfortunately, Tragedies will persist until The Good Lord returns. But even with everything that goes on in our crazy world, I encourage you, and may you take hope in this, as I say in the ending of this poem, Tragedies: someday there will be better days.*

# *Tragedies*

*W*hy's there so much misery today
drive-bys so children can't even play
we need to try harder to conquer this evil way.
All these crimes and tragedies
just make helpless people fall to their knees
this corrupt and vulgar way must cease.
Let us annihilate all the hate and lying
so people feel happy instead of crying
I know everyone's disgusted with the lewdness and dying.
One day we must change our ways
instead of feeling stranded like we're trapped in a maze
someday I know there will be better days.

9/4/2005

# Bible

*A lot of people feel uncomfortable talking about God, Jesus, and the Bible. And oftentimes when we hear people having "those kind" of conversations, we feel shaky and walk away, or we ignore it and change the subject. But just like talking about sex, drugs, alcohol, etc. (also conversations that make people feel uncomfortable), talking about God, His Son, and His Word is crucial, and is something we need to listen to and talk about. How ironic how we avoid difficult conservations and "touchy" subjects, when those are exactly the things we need to be talking about. I have no problem or worries talking about these matters, so feel free to talk to me about them if you see me. If you don't, feel free to talk to someone in your life - and we all have those kind of people in our lives - who you can talk to these things about. With love and care, I now give you this poem, Bible. And I hope that you open up your life to God and His Son Jesus, as I present one of my most powerful poems I've ever written.*

# *Bible*

*I*t's been around for centuries – to those who haven't read it, it's time to come aboard

the book is inspired by God Himself, and it's sharper than any two-edged sword.
To those who haven't read it, who haven't been introduced, or who let it collect dust
for the sake of your eternal destiny, I beseech you, it's time to read it, you must.
I've heard a lot – "I don't understand it, it makes no sense, it's just not for me,"
but it's for all of us – you and me – and once you delve into it your heart will see.
With concern, love, and care, now in short detail I'm going to walk you through
this awesome Word of God's, and how it most certainly applies to you.

*G*enesis, the beginning, tells the story of how people like you and I were first created

the book of Exodus, "going out," tells of hardship, but on God, still people waited.
The next book, Leviticus, is a guideline to how each of us should be living holy
Numbers may seem boring, but in it people grew, even when they started out slowly.
Remembering history comes Deuteronomy, and highlighted in it is rededication
next is the book of Joshua, where lands are conquered and birthed is a mighty nation.
Even when we turn from good, God still forgives, as the book of Judges shows
when hard times come, we need not fear, for Ruth rose above her lows.
The people wanted one, so coronated in 1 Samuel is Israel's first ever king
2 Samuel tells of David, a man after God's own heart, but even his sins brought sting.
Next, 1 Kings speaks of Solomon, the wisest man, and of Elijah the great prophet
following is 2 Kings – some were good – but many were evil, seeking only to gain profit.
1 Chronicles takes a look back at the nation's history, both good and bad
we can relate to this, 2 Chronicles mentions down times, but also times to be glad.
Talk about keeping promises, in the book Ezra, God's people return to their land
exiled from it they had been because of sin, but in Nehemiah they get a helping hand.
In Esther we read of a woman who was a hero to her people, as she rose to a queen
a man who suffers terribly but is later restored, it's sad all the things that Job had seen.
Like poetry? The book of Psalms expresses songs and prayers that come from the heart
closely following is Proverbs, which will open your understanding and make you smart.
Ecclesiastes wastes no time telling it as it is, for it speaks of absolute truth
Song of Songs is an intimate love story, told by Solomon most likely during his youth.
Enter the prophets: Isaiah speaks of a child born to us, a Prince of Peace
then onto the "Weeping Prophet", Jeremiah, whose faithfulness wouldn't cease.
Next up is Lamentations, Jeremiah's funeral song for his lost and fallen city
onto Ezekiel, a priest who ministered, and some of his messages weren't pretty.
We all remember Daniel, the prophet who was saved from the mouths of lions
and Hosea – his wife's unfaithfulness wasn't beautiful and bright as dandelions.

155

*Enter the minor prophets: they start with Hosea, and following is Joel*
*Amos then tells us of a complacent people, who sat back and were full.*
*Our next prophet is Obadiah, his book is the shortest of The Old Testament*
*Jonah was swallowed by a great fish, and for three days inside of it he spent.*
*The prophet Micah shouts judgment, but also of forgiveness to those who repent*
*batting next is Nahum, another of God's minor prophets who was sent.*
*Habakkuk tells us God's still in control of the world, no matter how dismal it seems*
*return to the Lord is Zephaniah's message, instead of following after worthless dreams.*
*Off the bench is Haggai, a postexilic prophet who tells us we still have work to do*
*offering words of encouragement that we all need, Zechariah names quite a few.*
*Last but not least of these minor prophets is Malachi, which finalizes the book of old*
*then it's onto The New Testament, that speaks of words more valuable than gold.*
*Enter Jesus Christ: Matthew, one of his disciples, is the first New Testament book*
*Mark records more miracles than any other Gospel, and you should take a look.*
*The Greek physician, Luke, is a New Testament author who happens to be a Gentile*
*John, the last Gospel, proves Jesus is the Son of God, and he has a unique writing style.*
*In Acts the church is born and we meet Paul, a persecutor who became a changed man*
*starting with Romans, letters are written to churches, and believers grow and expand.*
*1 Corinthians tells of problems in their church, and yes, churches have issues too*
*none are perfect but neither are we, as 2 Corinthians shows us that this is true.*
*Galatians speaks of genuine freedom for both the believing Gentile and Jew*
*in Ephesians we read of a powerful armor to be worn, no matter what we go through.*
*Philippians, a powerful letter, preaches the Lord Jesus Christ who is risen*
*serving next is Colossians, which is one of four letters Paul wrote from prison.*
*In 1 Thessalonians, we are told of a resurrection and of a church that was young*
*2 Thessalonians clears up timing confusion, but this church was far from dumb.*
*We meet Paul's true son in the faith in 1 Timothy, who was a close companion*
*2 Timothy follows, and Paul's love for Timothy was deeper than the Grand Canyon.*
*On stage next is Titus, from which we can learn that we all have a responsibility*
*slave or free, Philemon teaches of a true brother, as well as the importance of humility.*
*Hebrews gives us the definition of faith, the heroes of it, and listed are their names*
*and then James, Jesus' brother, tells us how our tameless tongues are like flames.*
*1 Peter – the disciple who denied Christ three times – encourages those who suffer*
*its twin, 2 Peter, is next – and this "rock" was forgiven, repentance made him tougher.*
*The first of three, 1 John teaches us that God is life, God is love, and God is light*
*John was "the disciple Jesus loved", and in 2 John we are to hold on to love tight.*
*In his last epistle, 3 John, he speaks of hospitality as he writes to a dear friend*
*Jude urges us to show mercy, pray, and to build one another up until the very end.*
*The Bible's last book, Revelation, tells of our world's end, it's time we changed our tune*
*but this book ends in hope, where Jesus says victoriously, "Yes, I am coming soon!"*

*I*n short, here's the entire Bible laid out for you, in the hope you will see

*that it was meant to be read, studied, and applied – I'm praying that you'll agree.*
*Still don't think it's for you? Well, the Bible is filled with stories you can relate to*
*it is written in translations that all can understand, so you can read it straight through.*

*Start somewhere that suits you best, and before you know it you'll be surprised*
*how it touches your heart spiritually, for its truth is revealed, and in no way disguised.*
*This God-breathed book is for all people, of all time, regardless of your individual title*
*I pray you pick it up and allow it to change your life, God's living Word, The Bible.*

*6/22/2017*

# Misery

*I'm not sure what I was experiencing or going through when I wrote this poem, Misery, but from reading it, it sounds like I may have been mad or upset with someone. This poem goes to show that we all have "those times" when we're not happy with certain individuals because of someway they're acting, how they are, or what they're doing. We're tired of them, frustrated with them, and don't want to be around them. There's a good and true saying that I'm going to share with you: "bad company corrupts good character." So be careful who you surround yourself with. But, instead of hating and just being mean to such people, I've learned that these individuals are in need of love and prayer the most. It's easy to be like most of the world and be callous and cold toward people who have wronged us or who we just don't like, but loving such individuals is a true test that will define what kind of person we are. I'm not saying you got to be overly kind and mingle with such people, but forgive from the heart and move on.*

# Misery

What's wrong with people this day in age?
acting cruel and twisted with all this rage.
Can't trust anybody, most talk behind your back
I don't understand what is up with that.
All these two-faced people I can't stand
to these people I won't lend a helping hand.
It's sick how people go about lying
lots of people can't take it and break down crying.
All this misery, all this evil
just causes a major upheaval.
Sad because people live this way till it's their demise
I'll never follow these individuals, I will rise!
Talk behind my back, I don't care
I know your kind, you're not fair.
Instead you're selfish and cruel
you people are heartless and have no soul.
Your jealousy and wickedness you try to hide
but I'll remain strong, for I have the Lord on my side!
Lie, be vulgar, keep on living how you do
for the rest of my life I'm staying away from you.
I can't stand your people's pathetic and hateful ways
keep away from me, I don't want to see you the rest of my days.

2002 or 2003

# Christmas Day

*I know, I've already written one poem about this holiday, Christmas Feeling, but I had to place this poem in this book too, because this is actually the first piece of work I wrote dedicated to Christmas. I was only 15 or 16 when I wrote this, but this season apparently was so important to me back then, just as it still is today. Reading about snow, caroling, Christmas trees, presents, giving, thankfulness, and of course - those delicious cookies - puts us in a good mood. Although I'm sure there are some who despise this time of year, I have yet to meet someone who utterly does. This holiday means something to all of us, but to me it's all about Jesus Christ, His Savior-birth into our world, and reflecting on what He has done for me. This is the meaning of CHRISTmas, so God bless you and enjoy, as the famous song says, this "most wonderful time of the year!"*

# Christmas Day

*O*ne of the best days is Christmas day
out in the white snow children play.
Christmas carols being sung from the town
it spreads throughout the community all around.
Many making snow angels as they lay
inside homes, trees are decorated in a different way.
Christmas Eve children hurry to bed
fantasizing the presents they're going to shred.
All the presents, all the toys
Santa bringing gifts to all the girls and boys.
Christmas is not a time for fuss
always remember to celebrate the birth of Jesus!
Christmas is a time for receiving and thanksgiving
it's such a heartfelt season for the living.
It's a time to rest from jobs, even bookies
make sure you leave that jolly old fat man some cookies!
Don't sneak for your presents, it's none of your business
God bless, and have yourself a merry little Christmas!

*2002 or 2003*

# To Be Left Alone

*Silent, down, no one around, blue, all by yourself -*
*these words can describe how someone feels when*
*they're all alone. Of course we all enjoy our "alone*
*time", but there's a distinct difference between*
*enjoying time to ourselves and being all by our self*
*with nobody around. In these times we feel a sense*
*of desolation, not a soul cares about us, and*
*nobody, not even for a moment, can understand*
*what we're feeling or going through. We've all had*
*times in our lives where we've felt this way, and*
*maybe not like others have, but we've all felt some*
*time in our lives a sense of loneliness. I believe To*
*Be Left Alone feels this way because we were*
*created for the opposite of this: relationship! So to*
*offer words of encouragement, I say, "You are not*
*alone or the only one who has felt this way before.*
*We all have. So open your eyes and heart and know*
*that there are people out there who care about you,*
*want to be around you, and who love you just the*
*way you are." Plus, cheer up! My poem, I Care, is*
*just around the corner.*

# To Be Left Alone

Nobody likes to be left alone
all silent, stranded on your own.
Right now you're probably feeling stressed
but keep your head up friend, for you are blessed!
No person to tend or be there with you
you feel there's nothing that you can do.
Your heart feels like it is broken
let those weighted feelings flee into the open.
Feeling set apart and sad
I'm sorry for the pain you've had.
All the pain, you must feel like a mess
but think positive, and give your head a rest.
Let those hard times forever be erased
breathe in new life, here's a foretaste.
Sorry that you've been ignored and on your own
I'm sorry that you know how it feels to be left alone.

*2002 or 2003*

# I Care

*And now we come to my final poem, I Care. Like a fairy tale story, I wanted to end on a positive and good note. We all feel different emotions, and sometimes the world can be so cold and indifferent that it makes us feel lonesome, lost, like no one cares or understands, or so many other things that would take up too many pages for me to write down. But I Care, and I always will, because the world needs salt, light, positivity, a caring attitude, and love. I too go through various emotions just like you, and it's always uplifted my spirit to have people who have shown care toward me. I want you to know that for you I feel the same. I hope that at the end of this poetry book something touched you spiritually, emotionally, or personally. As you close the final pages of Forever I Will Be, I hope something grasped your heart to make you want to pick it back up and read these poems at times. With a smile on my face and arms outstretched for a hug, I want to humbly say, "Thank you and God bless you!"*

# I Care

*W*hen life gets hard and you feel on your own
or it seems no one cares, like you're all alone
   I want you to know, I care.

*W*hen people don't seem to understand
or if no one offers you a helping hand
   I want you to know, I'll be there.

*W*hen you're having a bad day
and absolutely nothing is going your way
   I want you to know, it is your stress I will wear.

*W*hen the world is harsh and thinks God is dead
and compassion it withholds, refusing to let love spread
   I want you to know, for you I will say a prayer.

*W*hen others care only for self, hoarding their possessions
and money is all people care about, only adding to our depressions
   I want you to know, you can depend on me to share.

*W*hen you're sad, mad, unhappy, lost, hurt, or confused
and you need someone to talk to because your spirit is bruised
   I want you to know, it's your troubles I will bear.

*W*hen things, people, circumstances, and the seasons change
and when everybody and everything seems so different and strange
   I want you to always know with all of my heart, I care!

*7/1/2017*

# Acknowledgments

*Thank You God*
*Thank You Jesus*
*Thank You Holy Spirit*
*Thank you family*
*Thank you friends*

*Was anyone forgotten?*

# *About the Author*

## Jared McCann

*is the author of Marked for Judgment, his debut novel, and The Dead Will Rise, both works of fiction. Serving his hometown city of Mount Vernon as a firefighter/paramedic for over a decade now, the author enjoys and can always be found outdoors, woodworking, or doing just about anything. The proud owner of way too many pets, the author lives in his peaceful and warm country home in Knox County.*

## Find Jared at:

*Amazon:*
*amazon.com/author/jaredmccann*

*E-mail:*
*firefighterauthor@gmail.com*

*Facebook:*
*@jdmbook*

*Jared's author profile and books are available on Amazon (www.amazon.com). His books can also be purchased at Paragraphs Bookstore in downtown Mount Vernon.*

www.ingramcontent.com/pod-product-compliance
Lightning Source LLC
Chambersburg PA
CBHW032033040426
42449CB00007B/884